Place Me With Your Son

Place Me
With Your Son

The Spiritual Exercises in Everyday Life

The Georgetown University Press
for
The Maryland Province of
the Society of Jesus
1986

ACKNOWLEDGMENTS

Cover art, *Christ and the High Priest*, by George Rouault, reprinted with permission of the Phillips Collection, Washington, D.C.

Permission from the publishers of the following copyrighted material is gratefully acknowledged:

Centrum Ignatianum Spiritualitatis, Rome, for *The Spiritual Journal of St. Ignatius Loyola*, tr. William J. Young.

Scripture texts used in this work are taken from the *New American Bible*, copyright © 1970, by the Confraternity of Christian Doctrine, Washington, D.C., are used by permission of copyright owner.

"The dove descending" From "Little Gidding" in *Four Quartets* by T.S. Eliot, copyright 1943 by T.S. Eliot; renewed 1971 by Esme Valerie Eliot. Reprinted by permission of Harcourt Brace Jovanovich, Inc.

Permission to quote from *The Constitutions of the Society of Jesus, Ignatius of Loyola, His Life and Work*, and *The Spiritual Exercises of St. Ignatius: A Literal Translation and a Contemporary Reading* was granted by the copyright holder, The Institute of Jesuit Sources, 3700 West Pine Blvd., St. Louis, Mo., 63108.

Harper & Row, Publishers, Inc. for passages from *The Autobiography of St. Ignatius Loyola*, tr. Joseph F. O'Callaghan.

"Time after time I come to your gate" Reprinted with permission of Macmillan Publishing Company from *Collected Poems and Plays* by Rabindranath Tagore. Copyright 1916 by Macmillan Publishing Company, renewed 1944 by Rabindranath Tagore. "The Face of Christ" Reprinted with permission of Macmillan Publishing Company from *The World for Wedding Ring* by Daniel Berrigan, S.J. © Daniel Berrigan, S.J., 1958, 1959, 1960, 1961, 1962.

"Cantico del Sole" Ezra Pound, *Personae*. Copyright 1926 by Ezra Pound. "You, Neighbor God" R.M. Rilke, *Poems from the Book of Hours*. Copyright 1941 by New Directions Publishing Corporation. Reprinted by permission of New Directions Publishing Corporation.

"O shut your bright eyes" Copyright 1945 by W.H. Auden. Reprinted from *W.H. Auden: Collected Poems*, edited by Edward Mendelson, by permission of Random House, Inc.

David Higham Associates Limited for "I am the great sun" from "From a Norman Crucifix of 1632" in *Collected Poems* by Charles Causley; "Still Falls the Rain" from *Collected Poems* by Edith Sitwell.

"The Prayer of the Lark" from *Prayers from the Ark* by Carmen Bernos de Gasztole, first published under the title *Le Mieux Aime* and *Frieres dans L'Arche*, translated by Rumer Godden. Copyright 1947, 1955 by Editions du Cloitre. English Text copyright © 1962 by Rumer Godden. Reprinted by permission of Viking Penguin Inc.

Foreword

Popular reputation notwithstanding, Ignatius of Loyola was remarkably flexible in all that concerned the help of souls. This was certainly true in his use of the *Spiritual Exercises*. The preliminary annotations of his little book say that the *Exercises* ought to be adapted to the circumstances of the person who is engaged in them. In Annotation 19 he suggests that one who is suitable for the *Exercises* but "engaged in public affairs or necessary business," and hence unable to spend a month in solitude, may devote an hour and a half daily to the *Exercises* over a much longer period of time. From November, 1985, until April, 1986, Jesuits of the Maryland, New York and New England Provinces of the Society of Jesus chose to take Saint Ignatius at his word, and to follow the course of the *Spiritual Exercises* day by day, even as they went about their apostolic work.

The results of this Ignatian experience have been happy indeed for the men of our Provinces, so much so that many other Jesuits and friends of the Society have asked for copies of the handbook which was prepared to guide the three Provinces through the *Exercises*. This volume answers that request. It is a second edition of *Place Me With Your Son*. The present text has eliminated earlier references to the dates of our year of grace, 1985-1986. It now provides suggestions for prayer for twenty-four consecutive weeks. One may start these *Exercises* at any point in the year, although if the exercitant begins in mid-November, the pattern of prayer will coincide with the unfolding of the liturgical cycle from Advent to the Easter season. The references to the Constitutions of the Society and to the documents of recent General Congregations make it clear that this second edition still has Jesuits in mind, but I hope that it can be used with profit and some ease by other exercitants as well. Since it is a human instrument, not every page of it will be equally useful to all. In Chaucer's words, "Take the fruit and let the chaff be still," remembering with Saint Ignatius that the Creator and Lord in person is able to communicate Himself to the devout soul in quest of God's will.

Now I would like to thank the many people who brought this book into the light. It was the late Father Joseph Labaj who first invited the Wisconsin Province of the Society to make the Exercises in Everyday Life together. His successor as provincial, Father Pat Burns, kindly passed on to Maryland the booklet that had been composed in Wisconsin by Father Eugene Merz. The chief begetter of the present volume is Father Clement J. Petrik, chairman of a committee of Maryland Jesuits too numerous to name. He drafted the introduction and the body of the text, and then, in a wonderful exercise of the Third Degree of Humility, left the final editing to other hands. Father Terrence Toland, who, with Father Hugh Kennedy, had labored long to purge the first edition of errors, revised and expanded the text of the second. Both deserve special gratitude. My thanks also to Father William Walsh, who prepared and revised the references from the Constitutions and General Congregations of the Society. The treatment of the Examen owes much to material published by the Jesuit Center for Spiritual Growth at Wernersville. Aided by the indispensable Father Kennedy, Mrs. Agnes Muffoletto typed the second edition of the book as she had the first. And once again Father John Breslin, Director of the Georgetown University Press, and Ms. Deborah McCann, the Press's designer, helped guide it through the mysterious process of production. My thanks to them as well.

Saint Augustine once heard a voice that chanted: "Take up and read; take up and read." May God inspire us to take up this book, to read it, and then set it aside again and begin to pray.

James A. Devereux, S.J.
Provincial
Maryland Province of the Society of Jesus

July 31, 1986
The Feast of St. Ignatius Loyola

Soul of Christ, sanctify me.

Body of Christ, save me.

Blood of Christ, inebriate me.

Water from the side of Christ, wash me.

Passion of Christ, strengthen me.

O good Jesus, hear me.

Within Thy wounds hide me.

Permit me not to be separated from Thee.

From the wicked foe defend me.

At the hour of my death call me

And bid me come to Thee,

That with Thy saints I may praise Thee

For ever and ever. Amen.

Some Introductory
Observations

Some Introductory Observations

The Spiritual Exercises in Everyday Life

Saint Ignatius Loyola recognized that not everyone who wanted to make his Spiritual Exercises for thirty days had the leisure or the resources to do so. There were men and women who possessed the necessary qualities of mind and were drawn by God to the Exercises, but were tied down by personal commitments and the press of affairs. In Annotation 19 of his book Ignatius says that such a person "should take an hour and a half daily for the Spiritual Exercises." He does not say how long the whole process will last, but he does note that the same order of the four "Weeks" should be observed as in the book of the Exercises itself. This alternative method assumes that a director familiar with the Exercises will be there to guide the exercitant.

There are genuine advantages to be gained from making the Spiritual Exercises in the way suggested in Annotation 19. The experience strengthens the habit of regular prayer, teaches a greater facility in discernment, increases one's sense of the presence of God, and helps to integrate prayer and work. There are also drawbacks. It is difficult to set aside that much time each day; directors are not readily available; written guides to the Exercises in Everyday Life are difficult to come by. It is hoped that this book, without presuming to eliminate every difficulty, will make it easier to follow the Spiritual Exercises in Everyday Life and so to enjoy their blessing.

Time

Following the directive of Ignatius for "one who is more disengaged" (Exercises 20),* the full Exercises are usually completed in about thirty consecutive days. In the mode of Annotation 19 for those "engaged in

* References in this book to the *Spiritual Exercises* are to the numbers in the edition by Louis J. Puhl (Chicago: Loyola University Press, 1951).

public affairs or necessary business," the course is extended over several months. This book divides the matter of the four "Weeks" of the Exercises over twenty-four calendar weeks.

Some who use the book may feel the need to give more or less time to the matter of certain weeks. In this as in all things, one should exercise the freedom of the children of God and follow the promptings of His grace.

The text of Annotation 19 speaks of taking an hour and a half daily for the Spiritual Exercises. This includes not only time for prayer but also for preparation and reflection. Since the commitments of active Christians are heavy, some may not be able to give this much time to the Exercises. Others may be able to give more. A person may wish to divide the time so as to spend two periods a day in prayer. Whatever one's situation, all will want to make some sacrifice of time during these months in order to respond more generously to God's invitation.

Director

Annotation 15 says that "the director of the Exercises, as a balance at equilibrium, without leaning toward one side or another, should permit the Creator to deal directly with the creature, and the creature directly with his Creator and Lord." For Ignatius, therefore, God Himself is the director. Nevertheless, the human instrument may explain the process of the Exercises, give instruction in prayer, assist in discerning the various spirits, validate the exercitant's graces and propose further matter for prayer.

Perhaps the most important function of the director is to require of the exercitant a certain accountability in prayer, thus lessening the distortion that can come from the evil spirit and confirm those graces that come from God. Various modes of accountability are suggested here. A conversation with one's superior and spiritual director will be helpful to discover which one is best for oneself.

In the first mode of accountability one invites a trusted and respected person to be a director in the full sense — one who will assume responsibility for all the functions assigned by Ignatius to the director in the Annotations.

In the second mode one continues one's regular meetings with a spiritual director, but the conversations focus on the progress of the Exercises in Everyday Life and are more frequent than they would be in ordinary circumstances.

In the third mode of accountability two exercitants meet with each other every week in order to engage in spiritual conversation about the Exercises and to share with one another how God has been leading them in prayer. In this mode one partner, not strictly the director of the other, agrees to be accountable to the other in helping to discover God's ways.

In the fourth mode small groups of exercitants agree to meet regularly so as to share with each other what has been happening in their prayer, and thus act as instruments of God's grace for one another as they engage in the Exercises.

In the fifth mode a person makes the Exercises privately, setting aside an hour each week to review the graces granted by God and to keep some record of the various movements of the soul.

Written Resources

The first resource for this project is a copy of the Spiritual Exercises. Two versions are particularly helpful and are listed below in the bibliography. Louis Puhl's translation is perhaps the most readable of the English versions. David Fleming's version, *The Spiritual Exercises of St. Ignatius: A Contemporary Reading,* is described as a "companion" to the text. Using both these books will help one to understand the Exercises better and to pray over them more readily.

The second resource is the Holy Bible. Quotations from the Scripture in the present book are taken from the New American Bible. A commentary on the Bible, while helpful, is not necessary for the Exercises in Everyday Life.

The third resource is the present book. Besides introductory observations, it offers themes, graces and texts for each of the twenty-four weeks. Under the heading "Suggested Readings" are references to Scripture, to the Constitutions and to other documents of the Society. Many will have barely enough time for the daily exercises themselves. These readings are listed for those who have more time, or may wish alternate texts for prayer. Some may find it helpful to read and even to pray over the religious poems that are interleaved with the weeks of the Exercises. Certainly, St. Ignatius encourages us to engage the imagination and the feelings in our conversation with the Lord.

A final indispensable resource is a good, fat but easily portable notebook, wherein regular reflections on daily prayer can be recorded. For an example of St. Ignatius' own written reflections on his life of prayer, see the *Spiritual Journal of St. Ignatius Loyola,* translated by William J. Young. The work is listed below on p. xxii.

Structures of Daily Prayer

A day of the Exercises in Everyday Life does not differ a great deal from a Jesuit's ordinary day. There is time for daily prayer, for daily worship and for the daily examen. But during the Exercises we would wish to offer to God and to each other the gifts of greater intensity in prayer, greater awareness of God's presence, greater fidelity. Each Jesuit is asked to pray with and for the Province as all of us seek to respond to God's call in the Exercises.

The daily Eucharist is the concrete source of a Jesuit's life. During the Exercises one is asked to make a conscious effort to link the liturgy with the themes of the retreat insofar as this is possible without contrivance. It would be helpful if the celebrant in community Masses were to relate the liturgy and homily with the development of the Exercises. During the petitions of the Mass we should pray fervently for the Province, its men and its ministries.

During the daily examen one will wish to reflect on the Exercises of that day and on how one's prayer has been integrated with one's work and ministry.

A weekly reflection on our prayer following one of the modes described earlier is essential to the dynamic of the Exercises in Everyday Life. Questions and topics that may be raised during that reflection are given below in treating of the daily reflection after prayer.

Preparation for Prayer

The preparation for prayer takes fifteen minutes or less. It has to do with basic decisions and basic attitudes. During this period of preparation one decides where to pray, the posture that one will take in prayer, when and how long one will pray, and the subject of prayer. Normally this will be one of the scriptural texts or texts from the Exercises suggested for that particular week. One may wish to vary these with other appropriate texts from the Constitutions or other documents of the Society. The basic attitude in preparation for prayer is reverence. Reverence acknowledges that God is present to me; it governs my physical and psychic comportment in a way that befits the reality of God's presence. Ignatius tells us to begin every exercise with a preparatory prayer in which I direct all that I am and all that I do during that time to the praise and glory of the Divine Majesty. The preparatory prayer is never omitted.

Prayer Itself

Two things happen in prayer: what I do and what is done to me, what is under my control and what is beyond it. There are many things that I can control when I pray. I may read Scripture, listen to the words of Jesus, reason on the truths of Revelation, make acts of faith, hope, love, petition, gratitude, praise. I may be quiet and listen. I may sing hymns and recite psalms, I may finger my beads or pray the Stations of the Cross. I may engage in what Ignatius calls meditation and contemplation. The second aspect of prayer is what happens to me when I pray. In Annotation 15 Ignatius assumes that while one is engaged in the Spiritual Exercises our Creator and Lord can communicate Himself in person to the devout soul, and that He will inflame it with His love and praise, and dispose it for the way in which it could better serve God in the future. As we know, Ignatius teaches us to reflect on our experiences of prayer so that we may discern the various movements of the spirits: movements of grace in which we are drawn towards God, movements of the evil spirit in which we are led away from Him.

The meditations and contemplations of the Exercises are always pointed towards the grace and the colloquy with the Lord. Grace in this sense is something that I do not have that I really want and that only God can give. I do not bring it about in myself; I can ask for it, wait for it, accept it or reject it. The graces that Ignatius bids us ask for are all affective graces, things to be felt and experienced. In each prayer of the Exercises we are to persist in begging God for these gifts. The colloquy aims at establishing and confirming a personal relationship between the exercitant and the Father or Jesus or Mary. We ought to pray out of that relationship. The more the colloquy pervades the entire period of prayer, the more we grow in personal relationship with God and are disposed to receive what He wishes to give us. The various points and considerations for prayer are meant to help us develop dispositions that will enable us to enter into a loving relationship with the Lord.

Ignatius encourages us to persevere in the period of prayer that we set ourselves and not to lengthen it or shorten it. Fidelity to prayer in a dry season is often blessed with sudden grace. Ignatius also tells us to bring the formal prayer to a conclusion by reciting the Lord's Prayer or some other familiar vocal prayer.

Reflection on Prayer

After bringing the formal prayer to a clear conclusion with the Our Father or some other vocal prayer, it is often helpful to change position or place at the beginning of the reflection. Since prayer involves both what I do and what is done to me beyond my control, I try to capture these movements within myself and set them down in writing. Questions such as these may aid my reflection: How did God seem to me? What was happening to me? What struck me in particular? How did I feel when I was praying? What was my mood? Did my mood change? What was the Lord trying to tell me in all of this? Is there some point that I should return to when I pray again?

In his contemporary reading of the *Spiritual Exercises,* David Fleming interprets the text of 77 in the Spiritual Exercises, in which Ignatius gives instructions about reflection on prayer, in the following way:

> After a formal prayer period is finished, I should review what has happened during the past hour—not so much what ideas did I have, but more the movements of consolation, desolation, fear, anxiety, boredom, and so on, and perhaps something about my distractions, especially if they were deep or disturbing. I thank God for His favors and ask pardon for my own negligences of the prayer time. Often it is good to signalize the difference of this review of prayer from the prayer period itself by some change of place or position.
>
> I should spend about fifteen minutes in such a review. I may find it very helpful to jot down some of the various reflections that strike me so that I can more easily discuss with my director what has been my progress from prayer period to prayer period.

It is important to make this written reflection and review immediately after prayer, and to use it as the basis for the weekly account of one's progress in the Exercises.

Some Ignatian Forms of Prayer

Meditation is discursive prayer that employs the three faculties of the soul: memory, intellect and will. Ignatius explains his understanding of meditation in the First Exercise of the First Week (50). He does not mean that the exercitant is to apply the faculties of the soul in order, one by one. All work together, but the primacy belongs to the will, which has the first and last word. The subject matter of meditation is not abstract truth but the concrete realities of faith. In meditation we seek not simply to comprehend these realities intellectually but to savor them interiorly. Thus, the movement of this form of prayer is towards the love of God, a love which is given intimate expression in the colloquy.

Ignatius often uses contemplation and meditation as equivalents, but contemplation usually has as its subject matter "an episode of the Gospel, on which the gaze of the soul can pause, dwell, and find delight" (A. Brou, *Ignatian Methods of Prayer,* p. 130). Ignatius gives us a concrete example of contemplation in the exercise on the Nativity (110-117). Here, as in every Ignatian contemplation, we dwell on the persons, words and action of the Gospel text because they disclose the mystery of Christ the Lord, who died and rose again and is living still in His Church. We ourselves enter into that mystery heart and soul. Indeed, it is completed in us as members of the Lord's Body.

Repetitions and the Application of the Senses are characteristic of the Ignatian method. Ignatius usually presents his exercises of prayer in cycles of five. The First Exercise and the Second Exercise offer new matter which the exercitant must work at with some effort. The Third Exercise and the Fourth Exercise are repetitions and the Fifth Exercise is an Application of the Senses. The movement over these five exercises is from very active prayer which engages me vigorously to more receptive prayer in which I can peacefully allow the Lord to love me. David Fleming interprets Ignatius' directions in this way:

> Rather than take up new subject matter for consideration, I should return to those thoughts and feelings which struck me forcefully from the First and Second Exercises. I review those areas in which I felt greater consolation or desolation or, in general, greater spiritual appreciation. The idea of repetition is to let sink further into my heart the movements of God through the means of subject matter already presented. (Sp. Ex. 62)

> [The Fourth Exercise] is meant to be a repetition again—sometimes called a summary or resume. The hope is that the mind becomes less and less active with ideas since the subject matter does not change, and as a result the heart is more and more central to the way I find myself responding. The prayer period will probably be less active on one hand, and yet on the other by the grace of God it will grow in intensity. (Sp. Ex. 64)

[The Application of the Senses] is meant to be my own "letting go," a total immersion of myself in the mystery of Christ's life this day. . . . .It is not a matter of thinking new thoughts or of trying new methods of getting into the mystery. Rather the notion is to build upon all the experiences which have been part of my prayer day. Again it is akin to the passive way my senses take in sights, smells, sounds, feelings, as an automatic datum for my attention. The total felt-environment of the particular mystery of Christ's life, in whatever ways it can be most vividly mine, is the setting for the final period of prayer. (Sp. Ex. 122-125)

The Examen

The examen is a prayerful reflection on daily life that involves three special "times" or "moments." As I begin the day, I offer myself and all that will happen to the Lord. I remember the gifts of yesterday. I recall the area in my life of particular weakness and need. Once again I ask the Lord's help to cooperate more fully with His grace. As I move through the day, I take note of times when I've experienced some "movement of the spirit," some awareness of a gift from the Lord, some struggle within myself, or a "sting of conscience." As I review the day, I bring it to the Lord in a prayer that has five stages: asking, accepting, admitting, repenting, and resolving.

The prayer begins by asking God for the light and the grace to see my day from His perspective. I review the events of the day and accept them from the Lord, seeing where He has taken the initiative, where His grace has been at work. I savor again or for the first time how He has blessed, supported, and challenged me. I rejoice in the graces that I have cooperated with, and I take some time to grow in gratitude and praise to God.

I reflect on how I have failed to respond to the Lord this day and admit my failure. I see the times when I turned aside or backed away, when I fled or deliberately refused to respond to grace, times when I chose to follow temptation, when I lacked faith, hope and charity. As I return to this examen of "spiritual consciousness" each day, I look for patterns of vulnerability in myself, parts of my life where I see the Lord calling me to greater faithfulness and where I find faithfulness difficult. In all of this I monitor my choices and the "movements of spirits" within me.

I repent, acknowledging my failing and turning to the Lord for His forgiveness, focusing on my relationship with Him and on His patient love and His desire to strengthen and support me.

Acknowledging my vulnerability and my need, I resolve to be more responsive to the Lord in the coming day and to ask Him for strength where I most need it. I decide what I can do in particular to cooperate better with Him. I close the prayer with some personal gesture of commitment to the Lord.

Resources for the Study of
the Spiritual Exercises

BIBLIOGRAPHY

Begheyn, Paul. "A Bibliography on St. Ignatius' *Spiritual Exercises:* A Working-Tool for American Students." *Studies in the Spirituality of Jesuits.* 13.2 (1981).

TEXTS

Puhl, Louis J. *The Spiritual Exercises of St. Ignatius: Based on Studies in the Language of the Autograph.* Chicago: Loyola University Press, 1951.

Fleming, David L. *The Spiritual Exercises of St. Ignatius. A Literal Translation and a Contemporary Reading.* St. Louis: Institute of Jesuit Sources, 1980.

COMMENTARIES

Coathalem, Harvé. *Ignatian Insights. A Guide to the Complete Spiritual Exercises.* tr. Charles J. McCarthy. 2nd ed. Taichung, Taiwan: Kuangchi Press (197 Chunghsiao Road), 1971.

Cowan, Marian, and Futrell, John. *The Spiritual Exercises of St. Ignatius of Loyola: A Handbook for Directors.* New York: Le Jacq Publishing, 1982.

English, John. *Spiritual Freedom: From an Experience of the Ignatian Exercises to the Art of Spiritual Direction.* Guelph, Ontario: Loyola House, 1973.

Peters, William A. *The Spiritual Exercises of St. Ignatius: Exposition and Interpretation.* 2nd ed. Rome: Centrum Ignatianum Spiritualitatis, 1978.

IGNATIUS' OTHER WRITINGS

The Autobiography of Saint Ignatius Loyola with Related Documents. tr. Joseph F. O'Callaghan and ed. John C. Olin. New York: Harper and Row, 1974.

The Constitutions of the Society of Jesus. tr. & ed. George E. Ganss. St. Louis: The Institute of Jesuit Sources, 1970.

The Pilgrim's Journey: The Autobiography of Ignatius of Loyola, tr. and commentary by Joseph N. Tylenda. Wilmington, Delaware: Michael Glazier, 1985.

A Pilgrim's Testament: The Memoirs of Ignatius of Loyola. tr. Parmananda R. Divarkar. Rome, 1983.

The Spiritual Journal of St. Ignatius of Loyola. tr. William J. Young. Rome: Centrum Ignatianum Spiritualitatis, 1974.

THE LIFE OF IGNATIUS

de Dalmases, Cándido. *Ignatius of Loyola, Founder of the Jesuits: His Life and Work.* St. Louis: Institute of Jesuit Sources, 1985.

WRITINGS ON IGNATIAN SPIRITUALITY AND THOUGHT

Aschenbrenner, George A. "Consciousness Examen." *Review for Religious* 31 (1972), 14–21.

Bertrand, Dominique. "Un Corps Pour L'Esprit." *Collection Christus.* Rome: Centrum Ignatianum Spiritualitatis, 1974.

Brou, Alexandre. *Ignatian Methods of Prayer,* tr. William J. Young. Milwaukee: Bruce, 1949.

Egan, Harvey. *The Spiritual Exercises and the Ignatian Mystical Horizon.* St. Louis: Institute of Jesuit Sources, 1976.

Futrell, John C. "Ignatian Discernment." *Studies in the Spirituality of Jesuits* II/2, 1970.

Green, Thomas H. *Weeds Among the Wheat. Discernment: Where Prayer and Action Meet.* Notre Dame: Ave Maria Press, 1984.

Hassel, David J. *Radical Prayer.* New York/Ramsey: Paulist Press, 1982.

Rahner, Hugo. *Ignatius the Theologian.* New York: Herder and Herder, 1968.

Sheldrake, Philip. "Imagination and Prayer." *The Way.* 24 (1984), 92–102.

Whelan, Joseph. "Jesuit Apostolic Prayer." *The Way.* Supplement #19 (1973), 13–21.

The Spiritual Exercises
Day by Day

The First Week of the Exercises

The Second Week of the Exercises

The Third Week of the Exercises

The Fourth Week of the Exercises

The First Week
of The Exercises

The First Week of the Exercises

From the days of his convalescence at Loyola [Iñigo's] constant search was to put order into his life. He now realized that the first thing necessary was to know the purpose for which he had been created. What mattered most of all was to fulfill God's design for him. To do God's will it was necessary, above all, to know it. The obstacle was to be found in the "disordered affections" which obscure the eyes of the mind and drag the will toward sin. He would have to fight against these disordered affections, and for this he would have to overcome himself. This was the end to which the *Exercises* would be a help, and their title synthesizes their whole content: "Spiritual Exercises to overcome oneself and to order one's life without making one's decision through some affection which is disordered."

The work he was going to undertake demanded a generous and decisive will. Iñigo entered upon the Exercises "with great courage and generosity toward his creator and Lord."

Before all else, he placed before his eyes God's plan of creation: "Man is created to praise, reverence and serve God our Lord, and by this means to save his soul." The things of this world should help him in attaining this end. Hence it follows that "he should make use of them in as far as they help him toward this end, and he ought to rid himself of them in as far as they impede him from it." The truths of the Principle and Foundation are an orientation for the exercitant and a prologue giving light for the activities to be presented in the course of the Exercises—to such an extent that it is difficult to suppose that a document so important does not come from Manresa, at least in a rudimentary draft. Aided by the experience and studies of later years, Iñigo will succeed in giving it the perfect and harmonious formulation it now has.

In confrontation with God's plans rises the creature's rebellion, sin. Iñigo reviewed in his mind the course of his life, recalling the sins committed from year to year, the houses where he had lived, his dealings with others, the offices he had exercised. Two feelings overpowered his soul, shame and sorrow: shame for the loathsomeness

3

of his sins, sorrow for having offended God. But the result was not despair. "Imagine Christ our Lord before you on the cross, and begin a colloquy with him. Ponder how it is that from being Creator he has come to make himself man, and to pass from eternal life to death here in time, that thus he might die for my sins. I shall also reflect on myself and ask: What have I done for Christ? What am I doing for Christ? What ought I to do for Christ?" Iñigo's life will be an answer to this interrogation.

Another meditation on sins comes to a climax with a "colloquy of mercy," a confident and loving recourse to God's mercy, the sinner's only refuge.

Cándido de Dalmases, S.J.,
Ignatius of Loyola, pp. 67–68

Week 1—Introduction

THEME: As I enter these months of grace, I desire to dispose myself to experience the loving God as He chooses to give Himself to me. To this end I recall His love and His grace in my own history and in my prehistory, and I determine to let Him love me anew.

GRACE: I ask God to give me a more profound experience of His love, a deeper awareness of how I can respond to it, and a joyous freedom which comes from dedication to God's greater glory.

PRAYER:

A. **Isaiah 55:1-11**
God lovingly invites me to come to Him.
Psalm 63
I respond to God by expressing my holy desires to come to Him.

B. **Hosea 11:1-9**
His love for me is a tender love.
Isaiah 43:1-7
He wants me to be His own, for He has redeemed me. He calls me by name.

C. **Luke 12:22-31**
I am not to worry. My Father knows all my needs.

D. **Psalm 139:1-18**
In awe and reverence I remember how God has cared for me in times of joy and pain, in times of success and failure, in times of faithfulness and infidelity.

E. **Exercises 1 and 21**
Lord, I want to find your will.
Exercises 5
Lord, I want to be generous.

Exercises 22
Lord, I want to trust the Exercises of Ignatius as a way of renewing my life.

F. **Exercises 23**
Lord, I want to be unbiased and free in my service of you and your people.

G. **A review of the days thus far**
Lord, show me again what your gifts to me have been during this week.

Suggested Readings:

SCRIPTURE: Wisdom 7-9

EXERCISES: 1-20

CONSTITUTIONS: *Aids to Preserve and Develop the Society*
                813
                3, 134, 156, 826
                135, 136
                137
                138, 204, 243
                307, 510, 547
                603, 655, 719

> The Society was not instituted by human means; and neither is it through them that it can be preserved and developed, but through the omnipotent hand of Christ, God and our Lord. Therefore in Him alone must be placed the hope that He will preserve and carry forward what He deigned to begin for His service and praise and for the aid of souls. In conformity with this hope, the first and best proportioned means will be the prayers and Masses which ought to be offered for this holy intention through their being ordered for it every week, month, and year in all the regions where the Society resides. (*Constitutions* 812)

NOTE: The numbers above refer to places in the Constitutions (and later on in the General Congregations) which touch on a particular theme that relates to the Exercises. Each line constitutes a day's reading.

Time after time I came to your gate
with raised hands, asking for more and yet more.

You gave and gave, now in
slow measure, now in sudden excess.

I took some, and some things I let
drop; some lay heavy on my hands;
some I made into playthings and broke
them when tired; till the wrecks and
the hoard of your gifts grew immense,
hiding you, and the ceaseless expectation
wore my heart out.

Take, oh take—has now become my cry.

Shatter all from this beggar's bowl;
put out this lamp of the importunate
watcher; hold my hands, raise me from
the still-gathering heap of your gifts
into the bare infinity of your uncrowded
presence.

Rabindranath Tagore

Week 2—Principle and Foundation

THEME: Spiritual freedom is mine when I am seized so completely by the love of God that all the desires of my heart and all the actions, affections, thoughts and decisions which flow from them are directed to God my Father and His service and praise.

GRACE: I beseech you, Lord, to direct all my actions by your inspiration, to carry them on by Your gracious help, that every prayer and work of mine may always begin from You and through You be happily ended.

PRAYER: **A. Psalm 104**
The God who invites me is the God who created me and who made all else because He loved me.

B. Colossians 1:15-20
Christ my Redeemer is the head of all creation.

C. Wisdom 11:21-27
You spare all things, because they are yours, O Lord and lover of souls.

D. Genesis 22:1-18
The text of Abraham's faith and freedom questions my own faith and freedom.

E. Philippians 1:21-26; 3:7-16; 4:10-13
Here and now, how closely can I identify with the attitude of Saint Paul?

F. Repetition

G. 1 Samuel 3:1-18
John 3:22-30
Do I accept whatever He thinks good? Do I want Him to grow greater?

8

Suggested Readings:

For the preservation and development not only of the body or exterior of the Society but also of its spirit, and for the attainment of the objective it seeks, which is to aid souls to reach their ultimate and supernatural end, the means which unite the human instrument with God and so dispose it that it may be wielded dexterously by His divine hand are more effective than those which equip it in relation to men. Such means are, for example, goodness and virtue, and especially charity, and a pure intention of the divine service, and familiarity with God our Lord in spiritual exercises of devotion, and sincere zeal for souls for the sake of glory to Him who created and redeemed them and not for any other benefit. Thus it appears that care should be taken in general that all the members of the Society may devote themselves to the solid and perfect virtues and to spiritual pursuits, and attach greater importance to them than to learning and other natural and human gifts. For they are the interior gifts which make those exterior means effective toward the end which is sought. (*Constitutions* 813)

God be in my head,
And in my understanding;
God be in mine eyes,
And in my looking;
God be in my mouth,
And in my speaking;
God be in my heart,
And in my thinking;
God be at my end and at my departing.

Anonymous

Week 3—Sin

THEME: "What is it to be a Jesuit? It is to know that one is a sinner, yet called to be a companion of Jesus as Ignatius was . . . What is it to be a companion of Jesus today? It is to engage, under the standard of the Cross, in the crucial struggle of our time: the struggle for faith and that struggle for justice which it includes." (GC 32: 11-12)

GRACE: Conscious of the end for which I was created and of the vocation to which God invites me, I beg Him for a deep-felt understanding of my sin and of the disordered tendencies in my life, that I may feel shame and confusion, and so turn to Him for healing and forgiveness.

PRAYER: A. **Romans 1:18-32; 7:14-25**
I apply Paul's description of the Corinth of his day and his own personal turmoil to the situation of today.

B. **Exercises 45-54. The First Exercise**
With my eyes fixed gratefully on the crucified Lord who saves me I beg for the experience of shame and confusion, for the sinfulness of the world which God created, and for my sharing in that sinfulness.

C. **Exercises 55-61. The Second Exercise**
Grateful to God who continues to save me up to this very minute I ask to experience a growing and intense sorrow for my sins, and even tears.

D. **Exercises 62-63. The Third Exercise**
In the presence of Mary, of Jesus her Son and of our Father in heaven, I beg for a deep knowledge and abhorrence of my sins, especially my complicity in the sins of the world against faith and against that justice which is integral to living faith.

11

E. **Exercises 65-71. The Fifth Exercise**
Confident in God's unfailing love for me and grateful that He continues to save me up to this very moment, I dare to lie down as on the edge of a sea and allow to wash over me and fill all my senses the morass of evil which I have been contemplating, that evil whose fulness and consequence is hell.

F. **1 John 1:5–2:2**
"If we say, 'We are free of the guilt of sin,' we deceive ourselves; the truth is not to be found in us. But if we acknowledge our sins, he who is just can be trusted to forgive our sins and cleanse us from every wrong." (1 John 1:8-9)

Suggested Readings:

SCRIPTURE: Romans 1 to 4; 7:14-25
Ezekiel 16:1-22, 59-63

EXERCISES: 43, 70-90

CONSTITUTIONS: *Order*
340
360
816
817
821
659

All should make diligent efforts to keep their intention right, not only in regard to their state of life but also in all particular details. In these they should always aim at serving and pleasing the Divine Goodness for its own sake and because of the incomparable love and benefits with which God has anticipated us, rather than for fear of punishments or hope of rewards, although they ought to draw help also from them. Further, they should often be exhorted to seek God our Lord in all things, stripping off from themselves the love of creatures to the extent that this is possible, in order to turn their love upon the Creator of them, by loving Him in all creatures and all of them in Him, in conformity with His holy and divine will. (*Constitutions* 288)

An Hymn to God the Father

Wilt thou forgive that sin where I begun,
    Which is my sin, though it were done before?
Wilt thou forgive those sins through which I run,
    And do them still, though still I do deplore?
When thou hast done, thou hast not done,
    For I have more.

Wilt thou forgive that sin by which I won
    Others to sin? and made my sin their door?
Wilt thou forgive that sin which I did shun
    A year or two, but wallowed in a score?
When thou hast done, thou hast not done,
    For I have more.

I have a sin of fear, that when I have spun
    My last thread, I shall perish on the shore;
Swear by thyself, that at my death thy Sun
    Shall shine as it shines now, and heretofore;
And, having done that, thou hast done,
    I have no more.

John Donne

Week 4—A Sinner Loved by God

THEME: It is in the light of the Gospel that men will most clearly see that injustice springs from sin, personal and collective, and that it is made all the more oppressive by being built into economic, social, political, and cultural institutions of worldwide scope and overwhelming power. Conversely, the prevalence of injustice in a world where the very survival of the human race depends on people caring for and sharing with one another is one of the principal obstacles to belief: belief in a God who is justice because He is love. The way to justice and the way to faith are inseparable ways. Faith and justice are undivided in the Gospel. We are deeply conscious of how often and how grievously we ourselves have sinned against the Gospel, yet it remains my ambition to proclaim it worthily: that is, in love, in poverty, and in humility. (GC 32: 16, 17 and 36).

GRACE: In the presence of my Father in heaven, Jesus my brother and companion, and the Holy Spirit my consolation and strength, I ask for the gift of knowing my sinfulness so well that I may experience a growing desire for conversion, a new insight into the tactics of God's enemy and a renewed enthusiasm to follow Jesus.

PRAYER: **A.   Matthew 13:4-9, 18-23**
Reflecting on the parable of the sower, I ask God to let me see how deaf and without understanding I am, so that I may learn more about Him. I ask to see how shallow my relationship with Him is, so that I may allow myself to be more fully loved by Him. I ask to see what divides my heart so that I may direct it wholly and totally to Him.

B.   Matthew 25:31-46
I conjure up in imagination the circumstances of my death and judgment. How, when and where do I think my death will take place? If it were today, what would my unfinished business be? What would Jesus say to me at my judgment?

15

C. **Psalm 51**
   In this prayer of repentance I plead for the gift of God's mercy. I beg that He change me so that I live with a new heart and a new spirit.

D. **Exercises 313-336. Rules for the Discernment of Spirits, First Week**
   In the presence of God I ponder these guidelines and contemplate my own history. I ask the Lord to make me alert to the ways of the Evil One and to the ways of grace in my life.

E. **Repetition of D**

F. **Luke 5:1-11**
   At the moment when Simon, witnessing the miraculous catch of fish, was aware of his own sinfulness, he was able to respond realistically to the invitation of Jesus, depending not on his own worthiness or resources but on the graciousness of the One who called him as he was.

G. **Luke 15:11-32**
   I ask the Father to deepen my awareness and acceptance of His prodigal mercy.

Suggested Readings:

SCRIPTURE: Romans 5:1-11
              Romans 6, 8:1-11
              Ezekiel 36:20-36

CONSTITUTIONS: *Order*
                726
                260
                261
                263
                273
                822

All should take special care to guard with great diligence the gates of their senses (especially the eyes, ears, and tongue) from all disorder, to preserve themselves in peace and the humility of their souls, and to give an indication of it by silence when it should be kept and, when they must speak, by the discretion and edification of their words, the modesty of their countenance, the maturity of their walk, and all their movements, without giving any sign of impatience or pride. In everything they should try and desire to give the advantage to the others, esteeming them all in their hearts as better than themselves [Phil. 2:3] and showing exteriorly, in an un-assuming and simple religious manner, the respect and reverence befitting each one's state, in such a manner that by observing one another they grow in devotion and praise God our Lord, whom each one should endeavor to recognize in his neighbor as in His image. (*Constitutions* 250)

Discipline

Throw away thy rod,
Throw away thy wrath:
  O my God,
Take the gentle path.

For my heart's desire
Unto thine is bent:
  I aspire
To a full consent.

Not a word or look
I affect to own,
  But by book
And thy book alone.

Though I fail, I weep;
Though I halt in pace,
  Yet I creep
To the throne of grace.

Then let wrath remove;
Love will do the deed;
  For with love
Stony hearts will bleed.

Love is swift of foot,
Love's a man of war,
  And can shoot,
And can hit from far.

Who can 'scape his bow?
That which wrought on thee,
    Brought thee low,
Needs must work on me.

Throw away thy rod:
Though man frailties hath,
    Thou art God:
Throw away thy wrath.

George Herbert

The Second Week
of The Exercises

The Second Week of the Exercises

From the first division or "Week" of the Exercises Iñigo emerged as one already inflamed with love for Jesus Christ viewed as liberator and redeemer. Not only will he not offend him again; he will endeavor also to follow him. Christ appears before him as a king, whom he must obey and serve with greater loyalty than he has shown to the lords of the world. Jesus calls him for a great enterprise, the restoration of lost mankind. To him sanctity appears as the conquest of a kingdom, to be won by the victory over all enemies of God's plans. Iñigo knew these enemies well for he had been vanquished by them more than once. They are sensuality and carnal and worldly love. Iñigo resolves to participate in this campaign with the utmost generosity. He will have only to follow the example of Jesus, who will walk before him. His earnest desire will be to know Christ intimately in order to love him more and follow him. Meditating on the gospel scenes from the incarnation to the passion and resurrection of Jesus, he penetrated deeply into the divine Master's "intentions," that is, into his spirit and his principles, diametrically opposed to those of the world: poverty and humility against covetousness and pride. He will find everything summarized in the sermon on the mount, in which Jesus taught his beatitudes to the world. Iñigo will embrace poverty and humiliations in order to imitate Christ poor and humiliated, thus enlisting himself under his banner. He will follow Christ in his passion and death in order to have part also in the glory of his resurrection.

Cándido de Dalmases, S.J.,
Ignatius of Loyola, pp. 68–69

The Call of the King

St. Ignatius, though a remarkable visionary, was still a child of his age. He used the vocabulary and the images available to him to describe the extraordinary experience of God and Jesus which had been granted to him. That experience was one of profound, almost ineffable intimacy. The language of intimacy which this limping little ex-soldier knew was not that of a spousal relationship. In Inigo's world marriages were made for business and political reasons, and had very little to do with love, loyalty, fidelity, trust and commitment. But Inigo had known the intimacy between king and vassal, lord and servant. He knew from experience the covenant between the two, how each was ready to give his life for the other, how neither would abandon the other, how they would share the same lot, the same fare, the same struggle and the same triumph. There was a bonding which made them almost one in their lives, aspirations, disappointments and successes.

A network of such relationships formed a company whose members were united solidly under their leader. They shared with him and he with them the same enterprise, food, drink, clothing, work, vigil, toil and victory. To live or act contrary to this covenant was unthinkable for the leader, damnable for the vassal.

Jesus the King invites His followers to just such a companionship, one characterized by intimacy, and the sharing of a common task. The companion of Jesus the King grows in an awareness of who the King is, what He stands for, who His enemies are, what His aspirations and plans are. One grows in intimacy by experiencing the loving presence of this King who calls, teaches, heals, challenges, nurtures and accepts His followers as they are. The companion of Jesus the King yearns to bear with Jesus all wrongs, abuse and poverty if that is what is required for intimate fellowship with Him. One knows that one is never alone in the enterprise. One is in constant communion with the King in work, prayer, and rest. The follower of the King shares totally in the mission of Jesus: to bring the good news of salvation, liberation, justice and peace to all peoples.

Week 5—The Call and the Coming of the King

THEME: Speaking to the Fathers of the Thirty-third General Congregation on September 2, 1983, Pope John Paul II said: "Your
vocation consists precisely in seeking to follow Christ, Redeemer of the world, by being His collaborators in the
redemption of the entire world; consequently you should excel
in the service of the Divine King, as stated in the offering that
concludes the Contemplation on the Kingdom of Christ in the
Spiritual Exercises of Saint Ignatius." In its final document the
Congregation said: "Our religious life has been enriched by the
opportunity to 'labor with' Jesus in the greater service of the
Kingdom." (34) The call of the King is the call to companionship, to learning more about Him, to experiencing His loving
care and joining with Him in the service of His people. And this
King comes to us as one of us, all the more able to share our
lot.

GRACE: I ask the Lord for this gift: that I might be able to hear Jesus the
King when He calls and that I might be ready and willing to do
what He asks. I beg further for the gift of companionship with
Jesus such that my awareness of Him will become more
profound, my experience of His love will become more intense,
my union with His saving mission will be daily more
intimate.

PRAYER: **A. Exercises 91-100, The Kingdom of Christ**
I follow the development given by Ignatius.

B. Repetition of A

C. Micah 5:1-4
A mighty king will come to feed his flock with the power of
Yahweh.

D. Exercises 101-109, The Incarnation

This contemplation offers two viewpoints: that of the Holy Trinity and that of Mary of Nazareth. Here I try to see the world from the perspective of the Three Divine Persons and spend my time in the presence of God my Father, Jesus my brother and their life-giving Spirit.

> The Exercises invite us to contemplate the world of today with the loving gaze of the Three Divine Persons, that we may be drawn to understand its needs as God does and offer ourselves to share in His work of salvation.... Our contemplation of the world reveals a situation frequently hostile to the spreading of the Kingdom. The dominant ideologies and systems—political, economic, social and cultural—often prevent an adequate response to the most elementary aspirations of the human family at both national and international levels. A pervasive materialism and the worship of human autonomy obscure or obliterate concern for the things of God, leaving the minds and hearts of many of our contemporaries cold and empty. This both reveals and causes a profound crisis of faith that expresses itself in an atheism at once theoretical, practical and institutional. Lack of respect for a loving Creator leads to a denial of the dignity of the human person and the wanton destruction of the environment. Massive poverty and hunger, brutal oppression and discrimination, a frightening arms race and the nuclear threat: all offer evidence of sin in human hearts and in the core of contemporary society. (GC 33:37-38)

Feel the leap of joy in the heart of God when the decision was made to save this sinful world by the coming to us of the Son.

E. Exercises 101-109, 262, The Annunciation
Luke 1:26-38

Having already willed that the Son labor for the salvation of His people, God the Father now invites the collaboration of Mary in the mystery of the Incarnation. Though able to say "no," Mary freely said "yes." Present to this scene, I fix my attention on her and on Jesus, who has now become one of us for our salvation.

F.   Philippians 2:5-11

As I compose myself in the presence of the Trinity who determine that the Son is to become one of us, and as I contemplate Jesus present in the womb of Mary, I let this ancient Christological hymn express the awesome mystery of God the infinite become finite, the unlimited limited, pure spirit enfleshed.

G.   Review of the preceding days

Lord, show me again what your gift has been to me this week.

Suggested Readings:

SCRIPTURE: Hebrews 1-2
               I John 1:1-4
               Psalm 72

CONSTITUTIONS: *The Magis*
                 547
                 602

> Although it must be the Supreme Wisdom and Goodness of God our Creator and Lord which will preserve, direct, and carry forward in His divine service this least Society of Jesus, just as He deigned to begin it; and although what helps most on our own part toward this end must be, more than any exterior constitution, the interior law of charity and love which the Holy Spirit writes and engraves upon hearts; nevertheless, since the gentle arrangement of Divine Providence requires cooperation from His creatures, and since too the vicar of Christ our Lord has ordered this, and since the examples given by the saints and reason itself teach us so in our Lord, we think it necessary that constitutions should be written to aid us to proceed better, in conformity with our Institute, along the path of divine service on which we have entered. (*Constitutions* 134)

I sing of a maiden
    That is makeles;
King of all kings
    To her son she ches.

He came all so still
    There his mother was,
As dew in April
    That falleth on the grass.

He came all so still
    To his mother's bower
As dew in April
    That falleth on the flower.

He came all so still
    There his mother lay,
As dew in April
    That falleth on the spray.

Mother and maiden
    Was never none but she;
Well may such a lady
    Goddes mother be.

Anonymous

Week 6—The Birth of Jesus

THEME: God intervened in the history of His people to become one of us and share our lot. In the mystery of my own being and in the story of my own life He is an Advent God, intervening to save me, to love me and to share my lot.

GRACE: I ask the Father for three things that I need and only He can give: a more intimate knowledge of Jesus who has become one of us; a more personal experience of His love for me so that I may love Him more tenderly; and a closer union with Jesus in His mission of bringing salvation to His people.

PRAYER: **A. John 1:1-14**
Using Ignatius' "Third Method of Prayer" (Exercises 258-260) I will pray over the prologue of John's Gospel and let God fill me with awe and wonder at the gift of Himself to me and to all His people.

B. Luke 1:39-55. Exercises 263
Contemplating Mary's visit to Elizabeth I try to be alert to the human and divine drama taking place. I am particularly attentive to Jesus present in the womb of Mary.

C. Matthew 1:18-25
Contemplating this mystery I enter into the feelings of Joseph and his struggle with law and love.

D. Luke 2:1-7. Exercises 264
Peacefully present at His birth, I receive Jesus with joy and gratitude as the Father's gift to me and to His people.

E. Exercises 110-117. The Nativity
Following Ignatius' directions for this contemplation, I let my fantasy dwell upon all the details of His coming among us.

F. Repetition

G. **Exercises 121-126.   An Application of the Senses**

This period of prayer is meant to be my own 'letting go,' a total immersion of myself into the mystery of Christ's life. It is not a matter of thinking new thoughts or of trying new methods of getting into the mystery. Rather the notion is to build upon all the experiences which have been part of my prayer. It is akin to the passive way my senses take in sights, smells, sounds, feelings, as an automatic datum for my attention. The total felt-environment of the particular mystery of Christ's life, in whatever ways it can be most vividly mine, is the setting for this period of prayer. (David Fleming, *A Contemporary Reading of the Spiritual Exercises*, p. 79)

Suggested Readings:

SCRIPTURE: Isaiah 9:1-6

EXERCISES   127-131 and 162

CONSTITUTIONS
  AND CONGREGATIONS: *Service in Humility and Obedience*
               General Examen 3 and GC 31:2-4
               282
               728
               83
               284 and GC 31:5
               84-85 and GC 31:7-9

The Society of Jesus, gathered together in its 32nd General Congregation, considering the end for which it was founded, namely, the greater glory of God and the service of men, acknowledging with repentance its own failures in keeping faith and upholding justice, and asking itself before Christ crucified what it has done for him, what it is doing for him, and what it is going to do for him, chooses participation in this struggle as the focus that identifies in our time what Jesuits are and do. (GC 32:13)

A Child my Choice

Let folly praise that fancy loves, I praise and love that child,
Whose heart no thought, whose tongue no word, whose hand no deed
    defiled.
I praise him most, I love him best, all praise and love is his;
While him I love, in him I live, and cannot live amiss.

Love's sweetest mark, laud's highest theme, man's most desired light,
To love him life, to leave him death, to live in him delight.
He mine by gift, I his by debt, thus each to other due.
First friend he was, best friend he is, all times will try him true.

Though young, yet wise, though small, yet strong; though man, yet God
    he is;
As wise he knows, as strong he can, as God he loves to bless.
His knowledge rules, his strength defends, his love doth cherish all;
His birth our joy, his life our light, his death our end of thrall.

Alas! He weeps, he sighs, he pants, yet do his angels sing;
Out of his tears, his sighs and throbs, doth bud a joyful spring.
Almighty Babe, whose tender arms can force all foes to fly,
Correct my faults, protect my life, direct me when I die.

St. Robert Southwell, S.J.

Week 7—The Showing Forth of the Newborn King

THEME: In times past, God spoke in fragmentary and varied ways to our fathers through the prophets; in this, the final age, he has spoken to us through his Son, whom he has made heir to all things and through whom he first created the universe. This Son is the reflection of the Father's glory, the exact representation of the Father's being, and he sustains all things by his powerful word. (Hebrews 1:1-3)

GRACE: I beg the Father so to draw me to His son Jesus now manifested to the nations, that my awareness of Him may become deeper, my experience of His love more intense and my desire to follow Him more passionate.

PRAYER: **A.   Luke 2:8-18**
          I yearn to encounter Jesus with the simplicity and the directness of the shepherds.

          B.   Matthew 2:1-12
          To be as perceptive of the signs of His coming and as unrelenting in my quest of Jesus as the Magi were: this is the gift I ask of the Father.

          C.   Luke 2:19-21
          Mary did what a Jesuit would wish to do: in her heart she contemplated the reality of Jesus and the significance of His name. It is the name that I, His companion, also bear.

          D.   Luke 2:25-35
          In this mystery I contemplate Jesus within His Father's house, there for all to see, a revealing light to the nations and the glory of His people.

          E.   Repetition

          F.   Repetition

G.   Application of the Senses

Suggested Readings:

SCRIPTURE: Psalms 63, 131

CONSTITUTIONS
AND CONGREGATIONS: *Jesuits Yesterday and Today*
715, 718, and GC 31:1-9
Formula 3(1), GC 32:11-13, 19 and GC 33:35-36
813 and GC 32:20-23
GC 32:24-25
156
GC 32:26-28
603-605 and GC 32:29

> Our Lord, with whose name our Society has been signed and
> under the standard of whose cross it desires to serve the
> kingdom of His love, is Himself the goal of human history, the
> point to which the desires of history and civilization converge,
> the center of the human race, the joy of all hearts and the
> fulfillment of all seeking. "Enlivened and united in His Spirit,
> we journey toward the consummation of human history, one
> which fully accords with the counsel of God's love: 'To re-
> establish all things in Christ, both those in the heavens and
> those on the earth' (Eph. 1.10)." (GC 31:16)

Mary

O shut your bright eyes that mine must endanger
With their watchfulness; protected by its shade
Escape from my care: what can you discover
From my tender look but how to be afraid?
Love can but confirm the more it would deny.
   Close your bright eye.

Sleep. What have you learned from the womb that bore you
But an anxiety your Father cannot feel?
Sleep. What will the flesh that I gave do for you,
Or my mother love, but tempt you from His will?
Why was I chosen to teach His Son to weep?
   Little One, sleep.

Dream. In human dreams earth ascends to Heaven
Where no one need pray nor ever feel alone.
In your first few hours of life here, O have you
Chosen already what death must be your own?
How soon will you start on the Sorrowful Way?
   Dream while you may.

   W. H. Auden

Week 8—The Hidden Life of Jesus

THEME: Therefore, since we for our part are surrounded by this cloud of witnesses, let us lay aside every encumbrance of sin which clings to us and persevere in running the race which lies ahead; let us keep our eyes fixed on Jesus who inspires and perfects our faith. (Hebrews 12:1-2)

GRACE: I beg the Father to draw me to His son Jesus so that with eyes fixed on Him, I may come to know Him more intimately, to experience His love more profoundly, and be more closely one with Him in serving God's people.

PRAYER: **A.   Matthew 2:13-22.   Exercises 269, 270**
I contemplate Jesus, a refugee from His homeland, totally dependent on Joseph and Mary for His human survival. And they depended so totally on God that even in dreams they discern His voice.

B.   Luke 2:41-50.   Exercises 272
Jesus finds the Temple a comfortable place. It is, after all, His Father's house. I want to be with Him in His youthful zest for the things of God, and I invite Him to be with me as I go about my Father's business this day.

C.   Matthew 2:23, Luke 2:39-40.   Exercises 271
Today, as I contemplate Jesus at Nazareth, I may wonder about such things as: When did Mary first tell Him the story of His birth—the crowded inns and empty stables? How did she teach Him about God the Father? How did the thought of His future mission take shape? Why did He spend most of the years of His life in obscurity?

D. **Luke 2:41-52**

They found Him in His Father's house. Where else would He be? Then He returned with His parents and lived under their authority.

E. **Repetition**

F. **Repetition**

G. **Application of the Senses**

Suggested Readings:

EXERCISES 135 *Introduction to the Consideration of Different States of Life*

> One way of considering the mysteries of Jesus' early life is to see the interpretative direction in which they point. The ordinary life of the Christian is exemplified in Christ's obedience to his parents in the ordinary life of Nazareth. But the call to service in the Father's house is already manifested in the mystery of Jesus' remaining in the temple at the age of twelve to the consternation of his mother and father.
>
> While I continue to contemplate his life, let me begin to examine myself and ask to what state of life or to what kind of life style is God in his loving providence calling me.
>
> As a kind of introduction to this, in the next exercise, I consider the way Christ our Lord draws men and women, and on the other hand, the way the enemy of our human nature enslaves. At the same time I may also begin to see how I should prepare myself for a continued growth in whatever state or kind of life God our Lord may be moving me to choose. (David L. Fleming, *The Spiritual Exercises of St. Ignatius,* p. 25)

CONSTITUTIONS
AND CONGREGATIONS: *Prayer*
        GC 31:213-223
        GC 31:224-229
        GC 31:230-232
        GC 31:233-236
        GC 32:204-211, 216, 237
        GC 33:9-16

Following the example of St. Ignatius, a Jesuit's life is rooted in the experience of God who, through Jesus Christ and in the Church, calls us, unites us to one another, and sends us forth. The Eucharist is the privileged place where we celebrate this reality. Only to the extent that he is united to God so that he be "led gladly by the divine hand," is a Jesuit "a man on a mission." In this way, he will learn to find God in all things, the God who is present in this world and its struggle between good and evil, between faith and unbelief, between the yearning for justice and peace and the growing reality of injustice and strife. But we cannot achieve this familiarity with God unless we set aside a regular time for personal prayer. (GC 33:12)

You, neighbour God, if sometimes in the night
I rouse you with loud knocking, I do so
only because I seldom hear you breathe;
I know; you are alone.
And should you need a drink, no one is there
to reach it to you, groping in the dark.
Always I hearken. Give but a small sign.
I am quite near.

Between us there is but a narrow wall,
and by sheer chance; for it would take
merely a call from your lips or from mine
to break it down,
and that without a sound.

The wall is builded of your images.

They stand before you hiding you like names,
And when the light within me blazes high
that in my inmost soul I know you by,
the radiance is squandered on their flames.

And then my senses, which too soon grow lame,
exiled from you, must go their homeless ways.

Rainer Maria Rilke

Week 9—The Strategy of Jesus

THEME: It often happened that on a bright day [Ignatius] could see something in the air near him; because it was indeed very beautiful, it gave him great comfort. He could not discern very well the kind of thing it was, but in a way it seemed to him to have the form of a serpent with many things which shone like eyes, though they were not eyes. He found great pleasure and consolation in seeing this thing, and the more he saw it the more his consolation increased. When it disappeared he was saddened.

Until this time he had remained always in nearly the same interior state of great and steady happiness without having any knowledge of the inward things of the spirit. During those days while the vision lasted or somewhat before it began (for it lasted many days), a harsh thought came to trouble him by pointing out the hardship of his life, as if someone was saying within his soul, "How will you be able to endure this life for the seventy years you yet have to live?" Believing that the thought came from the enemy, he answered inwardly with great vehemence, "O miserable being! Can you promise me an hour of life?" So he overcame the temptation and remained at peace. . . .

But soon after the temptations noted above he began to experience great changes in his soul. Sometimes he found himself so disagreeable that he took no joy in prayer or hearing mass or in any other prayer he said. At other times exactly the opposite of this came over him so suddenly that he seemed to have thrown off sadness and desolation just as one snatches a cape from another's shoulders. Here he began to be astounded by these changes he had never experienced before. . . . From the lessons God had given him he now had some experience of the diversity of spirits and he began to wonder about the means by which the spirit had come. . . . God treated him at this time just as a schoolmaster treats a child whom he is teaching.

41

He went to kneel before a nearby cross to give thanks to God. There, the vision that had appeared to him many times but which he had never understood, that is, the thing mentioned above which seemed very beautiful to him and had many eyes, now appeared to him. But while kneeling before the cross, he saw clearly that the object did not have its usual beautiful color, and with a strong affirmation of his will he knew very clearly that it came from the demon. For a long time it often appeared to him, but as a sign of contempt he drove it away with a staff he used to carry in his hand. (Joseph F. O'Callaghan, tr., *The Autobiography of St. Ignatius*, pp. 33-40)

GRACE: As a brother of Ignatius I ask God to let me share in the gift given to Ignatius of being able to recognize the deceits of Satan and to guard myself against them; and I also ask for a true knowledge of Jesus Christ, my true Leader and Lord, and the grace to imitate Him.

PRAYER: **A. Ephesians 6:10-20**
The spiritual war.

B. Exercises 136-148. The Two Standards
The purpose of this meditation is to receive insight into the strategies of Jesus and of Satan so that I may accurately discern the spirits which I experience. Satan tempts me not so much in my weakness as in my strength.

C. Repetition
I will especially consider three temptations in the strategy of the adversary: riches, honors and pride. I shall also ponder the three steps in the strategy of Jesus: poverty, insults and humility.

D. Galatians 5:16-25
I pray to know what it is like to be with and without the Spirit.

E. Repetition
During this prayer I will stress particularly the threefold colloquy to our Lady, to the Son and to the Father.

F.   Exercises 149-157.   The Three Classes of Men
This meditation is meant to help me assess my freedom
and generosity in making a choice according to God's call.
I pray that I may be free enough to choose whatever God's
grace may indicate as His call to me. I make again the same
threefold colloquy as in the meditation on the Two
Standards.

G.   Repetition

Suggested Readings:

CONSTITUTIONS AND CONGREGATIONS: *Obedience*
          715, 718, GC 32:11 and GC 33:43
          General Examen 82
          General Examen 83
          General Examen 84
          284
          286
          655, GC 31:282

> Whoever desires to serve as a soldier of God beneath the
> banner of the cross in our Society, which we desire to be
> designated by the name of Jesus, and to serve the Lord alone
> and the Church, His spouse, under the Roman pontiff, the
> vicar of Christ on earth, should, after a solemn vow of
> perpetual chastity, poverty, and obedience, keep what follows
> in mind. He is a member of a Society founded chiefly for this
> purpose: to strive especially for the defense and propagation
> of the faith and for the progress of souls in Christian life and
> doctrine ... (*Formula of the Institute* 3[1])

Note

From this time on through the Second Week of the Exercises it is important in the contemplations on the public life of Jesus to focus our prayer on the grace we beg for and on the colloquy. The grace will always be to know Jesus more intimately, to love him more intensely and to follow Him more closely. The colloquy in all the contemplations on the public life is the one described in the meditation on the Two Standards (147) and repeated in the meditation on the Three Classes (156–157). This directive is given in 159 and 160 of the Exercises. Thus, the colloquy appropriate for all the contemplations on the public life of Jesus is the threefold colloquy which begs the grace to be received under the Standard of Christ, first in the highest spiritual poverty, and even in actual poverty and insults, if that be God's will. For a treatment of this matter see the little book by Johannes Metz called *Poverty of Spirit* (Paramus, N.J.: Paulist Press, 1968).

The Windhover
To Christ our Lord

I caught this morning morning's minion, king-
    dom of daylight's dauphin, dapple-dawn-drawn Falcon, in his riding
    Of the rolling level underneath him steady air, and striding
High there, how he rung upon the rein of a wimpling wing
In his ecstasy! then off, off forth on swing,
    As a skate's heel sweeps smooth on a bow-bend; the hurl and gliding
    Rebuffed the big wind. My heart in hiding
Stirred for a bird, —the achieve of, the mastery of the thing!

Brute beauty and valour and act, oh, air, pride, plume, here
    Buckle! AND the fire that breaks from thee then, a billion
Times told lovelier, more dangerous, O my chevalier!

    No wonder of it: shéer plód makes plough down sillion
Shine, and blue-bleak embers, ah my dear,
    Fall, gall themselves, and gash gold-vermillion.

Gerard Manley Hopkins, S.J.

Week 10—The Mission Begins

THEME: Divided into three or four groups, the pilgrim with Faber and Lainez, they went to Rome. On this journey [Ignatius] was visited very specially by God.

After he became a priest he had decided to spend a year without saying mass, preparing himself and begging Our Lady to deign to place him with her Son. One day, while still a few miles from Rome, he was praying in a Church and experienced such a change in his soul and saw so clearly that God the Father had placed him with His Son Christ that his mind could not doubt that God the Father had indeed placed him with His Son. (Joseph F.O'Callaghan, tr., *The Autobiography of St. Ignatius*, p. 89)

GRACE: I beg the Father to place me, as He placed Ignatius, with His Son so that being His companion I may know Him better, love Him more and be more faithful in my service of Him and of His people. I further beg that I may imitate Jesus in the highest poverty and in being able to bear insults and contempt, provided I can do this without sin on the part of another and without any offense to God.

PRAYER: **A. Matthew 3:13, Mark 1:9, Luke 3:21**
Exercises 158 and 273, Point 1
Jesus, having pondered in His heart the mystery of the Fatherhood of God and the mission given to Him by the Father, decides to leave Nazareth. I try to be present to Him as He reaches this decision, shares it with His mother, makes His farewells and leaves behind all that has helped to form His human traits.

B. John 1:29-39
I pray for the transparency of John the Baptist's witness.

47

C. **Mark 1:9-11. Exercises 273**
At the moment of His baptism by John a theophany confirms His sonship and His mission.

D. **Matthew 4:1-11. Exercises 274**
The tactics of the adversary are to tempt Jesus not to evil but to be a Messiah of possessions, prestige and power, instead of a Messiah of poverty, persecution and powerlessness, as the Father called Him to be.

E. **Repetition**

F. **Repetition**

G. **Application of the Senses**

Suggested Readings:

CONSTITUTIONS AND CONGREGATIONS: *Humility and Poverty*
Formula 4(6)
General Examen 101-103
Formula 5(7)
Formula 6(9) and 516, 518, 520, 522
553, 555, 560
569-570
577-580 and GC 32:257-258

It is likewise highly important to bring this to the mind of those who are being examined (through their esteeming it highly and pondering it in the sight of our Creator and Lord), to how great a degree it helps and profits one in the spiritual life to abhor in its totality and not in part whatever the world loves and embraces, and to accept and desire with all possible energy whatever Christ our Lord has loved and embraced. Just as the men of the world who follow the world love and seek with such great diligence honors, fame, and esteem for a great name on earth, as the world teaches them, so those who are progressing in the spiritual life and truly following Christ our Lord love and intensely desire everything opposite. (*General Examen* 101)

48

As kingfishers catch fire, dragonflies draw flame;
As tumbled over rim in roundy wells
Stones ring; like each tucked string, tells, each hung bell's
Bow swung finds tongue to fling out broad its name;
Each mortal thing does one thing and the same:
Deals out that being indoors each one dwells;
Selves—goes itself; *myself* it speaks and spells,
Crying *Whát I dó is me: for that I came.*

I say móre: the just man justices;
Keeps gráce: thát keeps all his goings graces;
Acts in God's eye what in God's eye he is—
Chríst—for Christ plays in ten thousand places,
Lovely in limbs, and lovely in eyes not his
To the Father through the features of men's faces.

Gerard Manley Hopkins, S.J.

Week 11—Jesus Calls Me By Name

THEME: In the Gospels Jesus calls a number of persons explicitly by name. Contemplating these mysteries we hear our own name called and we try to discover what happens within us at the sound of His voice.

GRACE: I beg the Father to draw me to Jesus so that hearing Jesus call my name I may better understand Him, more intensely experience His love for me and more ardently desire to serve Him and His people in the highest poverty and contempt, if that be His will.

PRAYER: **A.   Luke 19:1-10**
Jesus called: "Zacchaeus, hurry down, I mean to stay at your house today." In this encounter with Jesus Zacchaeus felt himself called to a whole new style of life. I climb the sycamore tree and ponder my own call.

B.   John 11:38-44
Jesus called: "Lazarus, come out!" Lazarus heard himself called from death to life, from being bound to being free. Lying on the ledge in the tomb I ponder my own little deaths and all that limits my freedom.

C.   Matthew 16:13-18, 23
Jesus called Simon by a new name: "You are 'Rock.'" This call was a great gift and it made clear Simon's role in the community. But he still needed redemption. Jesus had to give him another name: "Get out of my sight, you satan!" Perhaps I can discover God's name for me. What is my role in His community and how do I still need redemption? What does it mean to be called "Companion of Jesus"?

D.   Acts 9:1-9
I ask what remains in me of Saul, rather than Paul.

E.   Repetition

F.   **Repetition**

G.   **Application of the Senses**

Suggested Readings:

The mission of the Society of Jesus today is the service of faith, of which the promotion of justice is an absolute requirement. For reconciliation with God demands the reconciliation of people with one another.

In one form or another, this has always been the mission of the Society; but it gains new meaning and urgency in the light of the needs and aspirations of the men and women of our time, and it is in that light that we examine it anew. (GC 32:48-49)

The Collar

I struck the board, and cried, 'No more!
                              I will abroad.
What? shall I ever sigh and pine?
My lines and life are free; free as the road,
Loose as the wind, as large as store.
    Shall I be still in suit?
Have I no harvest but a thorn
To let me blood, and not restore
What I have lost with cordial fruit?
                              Sure there was wine
Before my sighs did dry it, there was corn
    Before my tears did drown it.
Is the year only lost to me?
    Have I no bays to crown it?
No flowers, no garlands gay? all blasted?
                              All wasted?
    Not so, my heart: but there was fruit,
                              And thou hast hands.
    Recover all thy sigh-blown age
On double pleasures: leave thy cold dispute
Of what is fit, and not. Forsake thy cage,
                              Thy rope of sands,
Which petty thoughts have made, and made to thee
    Good cable, to enforce and draw,
                              And be thy law,
    While thou didst wink and wouldst not see.
                              Away; take heed:
                              I will abroad.
Call in thy death's head there; tie up thy fears.

                    He that forbears
   To suit and serve his need,
                     Deserves his load.'
But as I raved and grew more fierce and wild
   At every word,
Methoughts I heard one calling, 'Child!'
   And I replied, 'My Lord.'

George Herbert

Week 12—Jesus Teaches Me

THEME: The manifesto of the Kingdom is expressed in the Sermon on the Mount. Listening reverently to this discourse I allow the seed of Jesus' word to be implanted in me and take root.

GRACE: I beg the Father to draw me to Jesus so that hearing His word I may receive it, receiving His word I may live it and may more ardently desire to serve Him and His people in the highest poverty and contempt if that be His will.

PRAYER:

A.   John 12:44-50
I dispose myself to listen to Jesus, for in hearing His message I hear the Father.

B.   Matthew 5, 6, 7
Mountains are massive metaphors for the meeting place between God and His people. In the presence of God I listen to the words of Jesus, letting their power and His person transform me.

C.   Repetition or continuation of B

D.   Repetition or continuation of C

E.   Exercises 169 to 174, 189
In God's presence I let Ignatius teach me about the process of making decisions according to God's will. I ask the Lord to enlighten my mind so that I will know what He is asking of me, and to inflame my heart so that I will desire to choose it. (**Note:** The Fleming text of the *Exercises* may be more helpful in praying on these points than the more literal versions.)

F. **Exercises 175-188**
Again, in God's presence, I let Ignatius teach me about making good and correct decisions. I will pray as in E.

G. **Review**
I review the prayer of this week to discover how the Lord has been teaching me and whither the Spirit of God has been guiding me.

Suggested Readings:

CONSTITUTIONS AND CONGREGATIONS: *Renewal of Ministries*
    156, 603 and GC 31:365
    618-621
    622
    623
    624
    625-628
    629-632

The methods we employ and the activities we undertake should express the spirit of the Beatitudes and bring people to a real reconciliation. In this way our commitment to justice will simultaneously show forth the spirit and the power of God. It will respond to humanity's deepest yearnings, not just for bread and freedom, but for God and His friendship—a longing to be sons and daughters in His sight. (GC 32:82)

The Pillar of the Cloud

Lead, kindly Light, amid the encircling gloom,
      Lead thou me on;
The night is dark, and I am far from home,
      Lead thou me on.
Keep thou my feet: I do not ask to see
The distant scene: one step enough for me.

I was not ever thus, nor prayed that thou
      Shouldst lead me on;
I loved to choose and see my path; but now
      Lead thou me on.
I loved the garish day, and, spite of fears,
Pride ruled my will: remember not past years.

So long thy power hath blest me, sure it still
      Will lead me on,
O'er moor and fen, o'er crag and torrent, till
      The night is gone.
And with the morn those angel faces smile
Which I have loved long since, and lost a while.

John Henry Newman

Week 13—Jesus Heals Me

THEME: The healing ministry of Jesus is also a saving ministry. His concern is not just for the withered limb or the non-functioning organ. It is also that the one whom He heals may turn from sin and believe in Him. Entering into these mysteries in prayer, I present myself to Jesus as one in need of healing in body, mind and spirit.

GRACE: I beg the Father to draw me to Jesus so that in His presence my helplessness will be revealed and I can allow Him to give me His healing love. With this experience of His love I ask for a more ardent desire to serve Him and His people in highest poverty and contempt if that be His will.

PRAYER: **A.** **John 5:1-9**
Jesus' question to this sick and crippled man is, in my contemplation, addressed also to me. "Do you want to be healed?" I show the Lord my need for healing: my pettiness, my pride, my ambition, my need for security and control, my self-deception. Yes, Lord, I want to be healed.

B. **Mark 10:46-52**
I recognize in Jesus' question to Bartimaeus a question He puts to me. I sometimes hesitate to answer, trusting neither in myself nor in Him. "What do you want me to do for you?"

C. **Luke 8:40-56**
I beg Jesus to come to my home. I strive to touch the hem of His cloak.

D. **Repetition**

E. **Application of the Senses**

F.   **Exercises 328-336.   Rules for the Discernment of Spirits, Second Week.**
In the presence of God I ponder these rules devised by Ignatius after being taught by God as his schoolmaster. I reflect on my own experiences and the movements of the spirits within me as I ask the gift of counsel and discernment.

G.   **Repetition**

Suggested Readings:

EXERCISES: 337-344   *Rules for the Distribution of Alms.* These rules are a practical example of discernment.

CONSTITUTIONS AND CONGREGATIONS: *Poverty*
GC 33:25-29
GC 31:284-291
GC 31:292-297
GC 32:259-261
GC 31:292 and GC 32:262-263
GC 32:264-266 and 269-271
GC 32:281-288

Poverty, as the strong wall of the religious life, should be loved and preserved in its integrity as far as this is possible with God's grace. The enemy of the human race generally tries to weaken this defense and rampart which God our Lord inspired religious institutes to raise against him and the other adversaries of their perfection. Into what was well ordered by their first founders he induces alterations by means of interpretations and innovations not in conformity with those founders' spirit.   (*Constitutions* 553)

The Face of Christ

The tragic beauty of the face of Christ
shines in the face of man;

the abandoned old live on
in shabby rooms, far from inner comfort.
Outside, in the street
din and purpose, the world like a fiery animal
reined in by youth. Within
a pallid tiring heart
shuffles about its dwelling.

Nothing, or so little, come of life's promise.
Out of broken men, despised minds
what does one make—
a roadside show, a graveyard of the heart?

The Christian God reproves
faithless ranting minds
crushing like upper and lower stones
all life between;
Christ, fowler of street and hedgerow
of cripples and the distempered old
—eyes blind as woodknots,
tongues tight as immigrants—
takes in His gospel net
all the hue and cry of existence.

Heaven, of such imperfection,
wary, ravaged, wild?

Yes. Compel them in.

Daniel Berrigan, S.J.

Week 14—Jesus Challenges Me

THEME: Of the King's followers much will be asked. There will be the "one thing necessary" and the "one thing more." Pondering these challenges I look to see what movements are taking place within me.

GRACE: I beg the Father to draw me to Jesus so that I may hear and understand the challenge, thrill to the adventure and ardently desire to serve Him and His people, sharing His lot and His suffering.

PRAYER: **A.   Luke 9:57-62**
            I pray not to be a would-be follower of Jesus.

          B.   Luke 10:38-41
            Jesus says to me: "One thing only is required." The challenge to me is to be both Martha and Mary, the contemplative in action whose work for the Lord is animated by constant intimacy with Him.

          C.   Mark 10:17-27
            Looking with love on a good man whose life had been a model of goodness and fidelity, Jesus challenges him, and challenges me with these words: "There is one thing more you must do." I know what He said to the man in the gospel. I listen now as He tells me in my own context what one thing more is required of me.

          D.   Micah 6:8
            In the presence of God I let these prophetic words take root within me. "You have been told, O man, what is good and what the Lord requires of you: Only to do the right and to love goodness and to walk humbly with your God."

E.   **Repetition**

F.   **Repetition**

G.   I use the Second Method of Prayer (**Exercises 249-257**) as I pray the Lord's Prayer.

Suggested Readings:

EXERCISES: 238-260   *Three Methods of Prayer*

CONSTITUTIONS AND CONGREGATIONS: *Faith and Justice, and Atheism*
          Formula 3(1), GC 32:48, 96-99 and GC 33:52-53
          GC 32:100-107
          GC 32:108-110, 111-115, 127-129
          GC 32:117-118 and GC 33:49
          GC 33:41, 54-55
          GC 33:38, 40 and GC 32:68
          GC 31:31-32, 34-40

> Too often are we insulated from any real contact with unbelief and with the hard, everyday consequences of injustice and oppression. As a result we run the risk of not being able to hear the cry for the Gospel as it is addressed to us by the men and women of our time. A deeper involvement with others in the world will therefore be a decisive test of our faith, of our hope, and of our apostolic charity. Are we ready, with discernment and with reliance on a community which is alive and apostolic, to bear witness to the Gospel in the painful situations where our faith and our hope are tested by unbelief and injustice? Are we ready to give ourselves to the demanding and serious study of theology, philosophy and the human sciences, which are ever more necessary if we are to understand and try to resolve the problems of the world? (GC 32:84)

Batter my heart, three-personed God, for you
　　As yet but knock; breathe, shine, and seek to mend;
　　That I may rise and stand, o'erthrow me and bend
Your force to break; blow, burn, and make me new.
I, like an usurped town to another due,
　　Labour to admit you, but O, to no end.
　　Reason, your viceroy in me, me should defend,
But is captived and proves weak or untrue.
Yet dearly I love you and would be loved fain,
　　But am betrothed unto your enemy.
Divorce me, untie, or break that knot again,
　　Take me to you, imprison me, for I,
　　Except you enthrall me, never shall be free,
　　Nor ever chaste except you ravish me.

John Donne

Week 15—Jesus Nurtures Me

THEME: Hungry and exhausted, the King's followers cannot long endure in His service unless He gives them rest. I come into His presence to be refreshed with living water, strengthened with the bread of life and invigorated by His holy word.

GRACE: I beg the Father to draw me to Jesus so that I may become more aware of His concern for me and graciously accept His nurturing love. I want to be more passionate than ever before in serving Him and His people, sharing His lot of poverty and contempt if that is His will.

PRAYER: **A.   Matthew 11:25-30**
          With my heart longing for companionship and intimacy, I welcome the invitation of Jesus to share His rest as He shares my burden. I ardently desire to give myself totally to the love and service of Jesus and His people.

          B.   John 2:1-11
          I join Jesus and His Mother at the first of His mighty works in Cana of Galilee. It is a wedding feast.

          C.   John 6:30-44
          I believe that Jesus is the living bread, the life-giving water and I beg the Father to draw me closer to Him so that, eating and drinking, I may have new life.

          D.   John 15:1-20
          I am nurtured by my union with Jesus, my friend and companion. I pray this passage using the Third Method of Prayer (**Exercises 258 and 260**).

          E.   Repetition

          F.   Repetition

G. Application of the Senses

Suggested Readings:

EXERCISES: 210-217   *Rules for Eating.*   Consider these rules not just for their content but as a practical example of the process of discernment and living in the company of Jesus.

CONSTITUTIONS AND CONGREGATIONS: *Chastity as a Summary of Jesuit Life*
547
GC 31:243-249
GC 31:250-251
GC 31:252-258
GC 31:259-267

Our vow of chastity consecrates a celibacy freely chosen for the sake of the Kingdom of God. By it, we offer an undivided heart to God, a heart capable of a self-giving in service approaching the freedom from self-interest with which God Himself loves all His creatures. . . . We might simply add that celibacy for the sake of the Kingdom has a special apostolic value in our time, when men tend to put whole classes of their fellow human beings beyond the margins of their concern, while at the same time identifying love with eroticism. In such a time, the self-denying love which is warmly human, yet freely given in service to all, can be a powerful sign leading men to Christ who came to show us what love really is: that God is love. (GC 32:225)

Love (III)

LOVE bade me welcome; yet my soul drew back,
   Guilty of dust and sin.
But quick-eyed Love, observing me grow slack
   From my first entrance in,
Drew nearer to me, sweetly questioning,
   If I lacked anything.

'A guest,' I answered, 'worthy to be here.'
   Love said, 'You shall be he.'
'I, the unkind, ungrateful? Ah, my dear,
   I cannot look on thee.'
Love took my hand, and smiling did reply,
   'Who made the eyes but I?'

'Truth, Lord, but I have marred them; let my shame
   Go where it doth deserve.'
'And know you not,' says Love, 'who bore the blame?'
   'My dear, then I will serve.'
'You must sit down,' says Love, 'and taste my meat.'
   So I did sit and eat.

George Herbert

Week 16—Jesus Accepts and Bestows Love

THEME: It is likewise highly important [to remember] to how great a degree it helps and profits one in the spiritual life to abhor in its totality and not in part whatever the world loves and embraces, and to accept and desire with all possible energy whatever Christ our Lord has loved and embraced. Just as the men of the world who follow the world love and seek with such great diligence honors, fame, and esteem for a great name on earth, as the world teaches them, so those who are progressing in the spiritual life and truly following Christ our Lord love and intensely desire everything opposite. That is to say, they desire to clothe themselves with the same clothing and uniform of their Lord because of the love and reverence which He deserves, to such an extent that where there would be no offense to His Divine Majesty and no imputation of sin to the neighbor, they would wish to suffer injuries, false accusations, and affronts, and to be held and esteemed as fools (but without their giving any occasion for this), because of their desire to resemble and imitate in some manner our Creator and Lord Jesus Christ, by putting on His clothing and uniform, since it was for our spiritual profit that He clothed Himself as He did. For He gave us an example that in all things possible to us we might seek, through the aid of His grace, to imitate and follow Him, since He is the way which leads men to life. (*Constitutions* 101)

GRACE: I beg the Lord to choose me for the gift of the third kind of humility in order that I may find my own life more patterned according to Jesus, my God and Lord—always, of course, if this is to be for the greater praise and service of God. (**Exercises 168**, cited from Fleming)

PRAYER: **A.   Mark 10:17-22**
With love, Jesus looks straight at the young man, and straight at me.

66

B. **John 12:1-10**
Undaunted by the cynical comments which her action aroused, Mary of Bethany, with reverence and gratitude to Jesus for restoring her brother to life, publicly anoints His feet with costly perfume and wipes them with her hair. Present in the house at Bethany I reflect on my own reaction, my own measure of love for Jesus and my readiness to make myself a fool for His sake. I pray the threefold colloquy suggested in **Exercises 168.**

C. **Repetition**

D. **John 13:1-17**
I survey the hushed scene in the upper room as Jesus washes the feet of His friends. Then it is my turn. "Shall I wash your feet?" He asks me. I know that the washing will mean that I will have an intimate sharing in all that is His: His exaltation and His desolation, His triumphs and His tortures, His Tabors and His Calvaries, His death and His life. Am I ready to wear His garments? To love what He loved and embraced? What answer do I make to His invitation now? Again I make the threefold colloquy.

E. **Repetition**

F. **Exercises 165-168. Three Kinds of Humility**
Do I find in myself the desire to follow Jesus in the most intimate possible union so that His life and mine become one?

G. **Repetition**

68

Suggested Readings:

Coming from many different countries, cultures, and social backgrounds, but banded together in this way, we try to focus all our efforts on the common task of radiating faith and witnessing to justice. We are deeply conscious of how often and how grievously we ourselves have sinned against the Gospel; yet it remains our ambition to proclaim it worthily: that is, in love, in poverty, and in humility.

In *love:* a personal love for the Person of Jesus Christ, for an ever more inward knowledge of whom we daily ask, that we may the better love Him and follow Him; Jesus, whom we seek, as St. Ignatius sought, to experience; Jesus, Son of God, sent to serve, sent to set free, put to death, and risen from the dead. This love is the deepest well-spring of our action and our life. It was this personal love that engendered in Ignatius that divine discontent which kept urging him to the *magis*— the ever more and more giving—the ever greater glory of God.

In *poverty:* relying more on God's providence than on human resources; safeguarding the freedom of the apostle by detachment from avarice and the bondage imposed by it; following in the footsteps of Christ, who preached good news to the poor by being poor Himself.

In *humility:* realizing that there are many enterprises of great worth and moment in the Church and in the world which we, as priests and religious inspired by one particular charism, are not in a position to undertake. And even in those enterprises which we can and should undertake, we realize that we must be willing to work with others: with Christians, men of other religious faiths, and all men of good will; willing to play a subordinate, supporting, anonymous role; and willing to learn how to serve from those we seek to serve. (GC 32:36-39)

The Call

Come, my Way, my Truth, my Life:
Such a Way, as gives us breath:
Such a Truth, as ends all strife:
Such a Life, as killeth death.

Come, my Light, my Feast, my Strength:
Such a Light, as shows a feast:
Such a Feast, as mends in length:
Such a Strength, as makes his guest.

Come, my Joy, my Love, my Heart:
Such a Joy, as none can move:
Such a Love, as none can part:
Such a Heart, as joys in Love.

George Herbert

The Third Week
of The Exercises

The Third Week of the Exercises

St. Thomas More once prayed: "Good Lord, give us Thy grace not to read or hear this gospel of Thy bitter Passion with our eyes and ears in manner of a pastime, but that it may with compassion so sink into our hearts that it may stretch to the everlasting profit of our souls." In this week of the Exercises we would enter heart and soul into the mystery of the Lord's passion and death. The first followers of Jesus recalled these events in great detail and set them down hour by hour. We do the same, watching and praying with Him in His agony, conscious too that His passion is reenacted daily in the body of His poor and suffering people.

Note

Because of the intimacy involved during the contemplations of the Passion, it might be well to review some aspects of the time called "colloquy." Just as in human situations of taking care of the sick or ministering to the dying, our presence is often more important than our faltering words or awkward actions, so too *to be with* Christ in His Passion describes our prayer response at this time better than any words or actions. Previously we described the colloquy as the intimate conversation between friends. Now we open out that description to include the depth of feeling, love, and compassion, which allows us just *to be there*.

Sometimes, still, we may want to pour out our consolations, our temptations, our fears, our hardness of heart to Christ our Lord. In times of great need, we may find the intensity of our begging reflected in our use of the threefold colloquy. We should remember that faced with the suffering of the Passion we may have to pray even for the gift of letting ourselves want to experience it with Christ, according to the manner suggested after the Meditation on the Three Types of Persons, in the note [at 157] above.

An interpretation of "199 Note" in David Fleming,
The Spiritual Exercises of St. Ignatius.
A Literal Translation and a Contemporary Reading, p. 25.

Week 17—Jesus Is Betrayed

THEME:
There is ... [a] remarkable renewal taking place today in the giving and the making of the Spiritual Exercises, whose vivifying influence extends beyond the limits of the formal retreat into the daily life of prayer.

Not only that; fidelity to the Exercises energizes our apostolic action. It enlarges our inner freedom to respond readily to the demands which the service of the faith may make of us. It deepens in us the self-abnegation that unites us to Christ crucified, and thus to the poverty, humiliations and sufferings by which He saved the world. (GC 32:208–209)

Christ our Lord continues to labor in our world to save all men and women. I ask the Father to place me with Christ suffering in the world today.

GRACE:
I ask the Father for this gift: to be able to feel sorrow with Christ in sorrow, to be anguished with Christ's anguish, and even to experience tears and deep grief because of all the afflictions which Christ endures for me.

PRAYER:
A.   Hebrews 9:15-22
Christ arranges a new covenant. Like the first covenant it is made good only with the use of blood.

B.   Exercises 190-199, 289.   The Last Supper
As Jesus gives me the Eucharist I remember that I am Eucharist, that God takes me, gives thanks over me, breaks me and gives me as gift to His people to be His presence among them.

C.   Exercises 200-203, 290.   The Agony in the Garden
To follow Jesus in pain and humiliation, darkness and doubt in embracing the Father's will is my vocation as a Jesuit.

D. **Exercises 208, 291. From the Garden to the House of Annas inclusive**
The pain of betrayal through a sign of affection, being denied by him whom He had called "Rock"—this is the lot of Jesus which I am asked to share.

E. **Repetition**

F. **Repetition**

G. **Application of the Senses**

Suggested Readings:

EXERCISES: 204-207

CONSTITUTIONS AND CONGREGATIONS: *Union of Minds and Hearts*
813, 821, 655, 671, 673
GC 32:212-215
GC 32:216
GC 32:217-225
GC 32:226-234
GC 32:235-243
GC 32:244-254

> Is he determined and ready to accept and suffer with patience, through the help of God's grace, any such injuries, mockeries, and affronts entailed by the wearing of this uniform of Christ our Lord, and any other affronts offered him, whether by someone inside the house or the Society (where he desires to obey, be humiliated, and gain eternal life) or outside it by any persons whatsoever on earth, while returning them not evil for evil but good for evil? (*General Examen* 102)

I am the great sun, but you do not see me
I am your husband, but you turn away
I am the captive, but you do not free me
I am the captain you will not obey

I am the truth, but you will not believe me
I am the city, where you will not stay
I am your wife, your child, but you will leave me
I am the God to whom you will not pray

I am your counsel, but you do not hear me
I am the lover whom you will betray
I am the victor, but you do not cheer me
I am the holy dove whom you will slay

I am your life, but if you will not name me
Seal up your soul with tears and never blame me

'From a Norman Crucifix of 1632'
by Charles Causley

Week 18—Jesus Is Tortured

THEME: Availability for the meanest tasks, or at least the desire to be thus available, is part of the identity of the Jesuit. When he offers to distinguish himself in the service of the Eternal King, when he asks to be received under his standard, when he glories with Ignatius in being placed by the Father "with the Son," he does so not in any spirit of prideful privilege, but in the spirit of him who "emptied himself to assume the condition of a slave, even to accepting death, death on a cross." (GC 32:40)

Christ our Lord continues to labor in our world to save all men and women. He continues to be tortured in His body.

GRACE: I ask the Father for this gift: to be able to feel sorrow with Christ in sorrow, to be anguished with Christ's anguish, and even to experience tears and deep grief because of all the afflictions which Christ endures for me and for the world.

PRAYER: **A.   Isaiah 52:13-53:12**
I listen prayerfully to the fourth song of the servant of Yahweh as it echoes into the present.

B.   Exercises 292.   From the House of Annas to the House of Caiphas, inclusive
I pray with all the sincerity I can that I may desire to imitate Jesus in bearing insults, wrongs and humiliations without any offense being given to God.

C.   Exercises 293, 295.   Jesus Before Pilate
A frenzied mob, a pressured politician, a strategic scapegoat, a thorn crown and a reed scepter greet the King of Kings. I can at least stand beside Him.

D.   Exercises 294.   Jesus Before Herod
"Herod was extremely pleased to see Jesus." (Luke 23:8) Such irony contrasts with my own delight in my encounter with Jesus my companion King.

E.   Repetition

F.   Repetition

G.   Application of the Senses

Suggested Readings:

> In addition to superiors, there are also directors of works. Where fitting, and in accord with norms that must be approved by Father General, the director of a work can have true religious authority in directing the efforts of those who have been assigned to work in that apostolate so that everything may be directed to the greater glory of God and the progress of others in Christian life and teaching.(GC 32:229)

Still Falls the Rain
(The Raids, 1940. Night and Dawn)

Still falls the Rain—
Dark as the world of man, black as our loss—
Blind as the nineteen hundred and forty nails
Upon the Cross.

Still falls the Rain
With a sound like the pulse of the heart that is changed to the hammerbeat
In the Potters' Field, and the sound of the impious feet
On the Tomb:
         Still falls the Rain
In the Field of Blood where the small hopes breed and the human brain
Nurtures its greed, that worm with the brow of Cain.

Still falls the Rain
At the feet of the Starved Man hung upon the Cross.
Christ that each day, each night, nails there, have mercy on us—
On Dives and on Lazarus:
Under the Rain the sore and the gold are as one.

Still falls the Rain—
Still falls the Blood from the Starved Man's wounded Side
He bears in his Heart all wounds,—those of the light that died,
The last faint spark
In the self-murdered heart, the wounds of the sad uncomprehending dark,
The wounds of the baited bear,—
The blind and weeping bear whom the keepers beat
On his helpless flesh . . . the tears of the hunted hare.

Still falls the Rain—
Then—O Ile leape up to my God: who pulles me doune—

See, see where Christ's blood streams in the firmament:
It flows from the Brow we nailed upon the tree
Deep to the dying, to the thirsting heart
That holds the fires of the world,—dark-smirched with pain
As Caesar's laurel crown.

Then sounds the voice of One who like the heart of man
Was once a child who among beasts has lain—
'Still do I love, still shed my innocent light, my Blood, for thee.'

Edith Sitwell

Week 19—The King Mounts His Throne

THEME: Saturday (February 23, 1544)—While preparing the altar, the
thought of Jesus occurred to me. I felt a movement to follow
Him, it seemed to me interiorly, since He was the head of the
Society. . . . This thought moved me to devotion and to tears.
. . . I went along with these thoughts and vested while they
increased . . . and thinking that the appearance of Jesus was in
some way from the Most Holy Trinity, I recalled the day when
the Father placed me with the Son. As I finished vesting with
this intention of impressing on my mind the name of Jesus . . . a
fresh attack of tears and sobbing came upon me. . . . as I held the
Blessed Sacrament in my hands, the word came to me with an
intense interior movement never to leave Him for all heaven
and earth.

Sunday (February 24, 1544)—While preparing the altar and
vesting, I saw a representation of the name of Jesus with much
love, confirmation and increased desire to follow Him.

All through the Mass very great devotion, on the whole, with
many tears, and several times loss of speech, all devotion and
feeling being directed by Jesus. . . . Having finished Mass, I had
during the prayer that same feeling towards the Son . . . and felt
that it was given to me through Jesus, when He showed Himself
to me.

Later, at the fire, there was a fresh representation of Jesus with
great devotion and movement to tears. Later as I walked
through the streets, I had a vivid representation of Jesus with
interior movements and tears. After dinner . . . I felt or saw
Jesus, had many interior movements and many tears.

At these times, when I sensed or saw Jesus, I felt so great a
love within me that I thought that nothing could happen in the
future that would separate me from Him. (William J. Young, S.J.,
tr., *The Spiritual Journal of St. Ignatius Loyola*, pp. 15-17)

Christ our Lord continues to labor in our world to save all men and women. He continues to be led to His cross. I ask the Father to place me with Christ crucified in the world today.

GRACE: I ask the Father for this gift: to be able to feel sorrow with Christ in sorrow, to be anguished with Christ's anguish, and even to experience tears and deep grief because of all the afflictions which Christ endures for me.

PRAYER:
A. **Exercises 296. The Way of the Cross**
With some of His other companions I watch along the way to Calvary. I am grateful for the women who tried to comfort Him and for Simon who helped shoulder the cross. The hammered nails pierce my spirit.

B. **Exercises 297. Jesus Dies on the Cross**
"All his friends and the women who had accompanied him from Galilee were standing at a distance watching everything." (Luke 23:49) I join them and watch, listen, remember and ponder this mystery.

C. **Exercises 298. From the Cross to the Sepulcher**
Matthew 27:57-61; John 19:38-42
I join the small procession to the tomb.

D. **Repetition**

E. **Repetition**

F. **Repetition of the whole Passion**

G. I accompany Mary, the Mother of Jesus, away from the tomb back to the house where she is staying. I stay with her, I wait with her, I listen to her as she shares with me all those things she has pondered in her heart. I listen to her memories of her Son. I weep with her, I hope with her. And I tell her who I am.

84

Suggested Readings:

CONSTITUTIONS: *Humility*
             725
             Ganss, p. 309, note 1
             423
             250
             63, 93, 265
             577, 580

> The constant practice of humility ... has never been sufficiently praised. (*Formula:* 4[6])

O King of the Friday
Whose limbs were stretched on the cross,
O Lord who did suffer
The bruises, the wounds, the loss,
We stretch ourselves
Beneath the shield of thy might,
Some fruit from the tree of thy passion
Fall on us this night!

From the Irish

You prepare a banquet for me,
    where all my enemies can see me;
you welcome me by pouring ointment on
        my head
    and filling my cup to the brim.
Certainly your goodness and love will be
        with me as long as I live;
    and your house will be my home for-
        ever.

*This selection of Holy Scripture in Today's English
Version consists of Psalm 23.*

*The American Bible Society is one of 100 national Bible
society offices throughout the world whose goal is to
reach every person with a copy of Scripture in a language he can understand and at a price he can readily
afford. If you are interested in ordering additional copies of this selection (order number 06906), please write
to: American Bible Society, 1865 Broadway, New York,
N. Y. 10023.*

AMERICAN BIBLE SOCIETY
New York

EV 860P   ABS-1975-2,000,000-4,600,000-Q-3-06906-B

Psalm 23

The Lord Our Shepherd

The Lord is my shepherd;
    I have everything I need.
He lets me rest in fields of green grass
    and leads me to quiet pools of fresh
      water.
He gives me new strength.

He guides me in the right way,
    as he has promised.
Even if that way goes through deepest
    darkness,
    I will not be afraid, Lord,
    because you are with me!
Your shepherd's rod and staff keep me
    safe.

The Fourth Week
of The Exercises

The Fourth Week of the Exercises

"Praised be God, the Father of our Lord Jesus Christ, the Father of mercies, and the God of all consolation! He comforts us in all our afflictions and thus enables us to comfort those who are in trouble, with the same consolation we have received from him. As we have shared much in the suffering of Christ, so through Christ do we share abundantly in his consolation."

(2 Corinthians 1:3–5)

The consolation, the joy, the new surge of life that the Risen Christ bestows upon His followers from Easter morning until this present day is the gift we beg for in the Fourth Week of the Exercises. Hopkins captured Ignatius' thought in these words: "Let Him easter in us, be a dayspring to the dimness of us, be a crimson-cresseted east." In all of these contemplations we observe how the Risen Lord manifests the true splendor of the Godhead by consoling and strengthening those whom the Father loves.

Week 20—Christ the Lord Conquers Death

THEME: If we Jesuits wish to be faithful to the special character of our vocation, "we must 'contemplate' our world as Ignatius did his, that we may hear anew the call of Christ dying and rising in the anguish and aspirations of men and women." (GC 32:68)

The risen Lord is with us as He promised, to console us and to give us His gifts so that we may console those who suffer in the world today.

GRACE: I ask the Father for this gift: to be able to enter into the joy of the risen and victorious Christ.

PRAYER: **A.** **Exercises 219-225, 299. The Risen Jesus Appears to His Mother**
Having spent with Mary the day of Jesus' burial, I am now reverently present as Jesus comes. I listen, I observe, I speak, I pray, I touch.

B. **John 20:11-18**
With Mary Magdalene I hear my name, and respond with joy.

C. **Luke 24:13-35**
Jesus, my companion on my own journey to Emmaus, points out to me how He has been part of my history and prehistory. Consoled I want to proclaim to all: "The Lord has been raised!"

D. **John 20:19-23**
The fear, guilt, and confusion of the ten companions of Jesus in the room are familiar to me. I have felt them all. It is into just such a place that He wants and needs to come. I welcome Him and receive His five gifts: peace, joy, mission, His abiding Spirit and a forgiving heart.

E.   **Repetition**

F.   **Repetition**

G.   **Application of the Senses**

Suggested Readings:

EXERCISES: 352-370   *Rules for Thinking With the Church,* together
with GC 33:1:6-8, "Life in the Church"

CONSTITUTIONS AND CONGREGATIONS: *Jesuit Apostolic Community*
671, 273-274
GC 31:312-316
GC 31:317-325
GC 31:326-336
GC 31:337-344
GC 31:345-354
GC 31:480-487

Whatever helps toward the union of the members of this
Society among themselves and with their head will also help
much toward preserving the well-being of the Society. This is
especially the case with the bond of wills, which is the mutual
charity and love they have for one another. This bond is
strengthened by their getting information and news from one
another and by having much intercommunication, by their
following one same doctrine, and by their being uniform in
everything as far as possible, and above all by the link of
obedience which unites the individuals with their superiors,
and the local superiors among themselves and with the
provincials, and both the local superiors and provincials with
the general, in such a way that the subordination of some to
others is diligently preserved. (*Constitutions:* 821)

Most glorious Lord of lyfe, that on this day,
    Didst make thy triumph over death and sin:
And having harrowd hell, didst bring away
    Captivity thence captive us to win:
    This joyous day, deare Lord, with joy begin,
And grant that we, for whom thou diddest dye,
    Being with thy deare blood clene washt from sin,
May live for ever in felicity.
And that thy love we weighing worthily,
    May likewise love thee for the same againe:
And for thy sake that all lyke deare didst buy,
    With love may one another entertayne.
    So let us love, deare love, lyke as we ought,
    Love is the lesson which the Lord us taught.

Edmund Spenser

Week 21—The King Sends Forth His Followers

THEME: "When you send forth your spirit, they are created, and you renew the face of the earth." (Psalm 104:30)

The Father continues to pour out the Spirit of Christ on the men and women of our day. He consoles us still, and sends us on mission to console the suffering and the poor and all who long for salvation.

GRACE: I ask the Father for this gift: to be able to enter into the joy and the consoling mission of Jesus in His risen life.

PRAYER: **A.   John 20:24-29**
Tolerant of my dimness and unbelief as He was of Thomas, Jesus delights in consoling me with the gift of renewed faith. In His loving presence I utter, "My Lord and my God!"

B.   John 21:1-17
A moment of joy—"It is the Lord!" A moment of companionship—"Come and eat your meal." A moment of intimacy—"Do you love me?" A moment of mission—"Feed my sheep."

C.   Matthew 28:16-20
The men—those sinners He had invited to be His companions, along with me and others more sinful or more faithful than myself.

The mountain—that meeting place between God and His people. It could be a slum, a lab, a church, a clinic, an office, a parlor, a classroom.

The mission — go, baptize, teach, — at every moment, in every circumstance of life.

The promise—with you always: sinful, unfaithful, limited; every joyful and painful moment.

D. **Luke 24:44-53**
I join the disciples in receiving His commission and His blessing.

E. **Repetition**

F. **Repetition**

G. **Application of the Senses**

Suggested Readings:

CONSTITUTIONS AND CONGREGATIONS: *The Society and Its Superiors*
655-656 and 719
657-659, 662-664 and 666-670
671, 673-676, 677, 821
694, 700-701
719, 820, 723-735
820, 736, 765
820, 766, 768-774, 811, 822, 826

In all well-organized communities or congregations there must be, besides the persons who take care of the particular goals, one or several whose proper duty is to attend to the universal good. So too in the Society, in addition to those who have charge of its single houses or colleges and of its single provinces where it has those houses or colleges, there must be someone who holds that charge of the entire body of the Society, one whose duty is the good government, preservation, and development of the whole body of the Society; and this person is the superior general. . . . From what has been said about the general it will be possible to infer what is applicable to the provincial superiors, local superiors, and rectors of colleges, with respect to their qualities, authority, function, and the aids which each one ought to have. (*Constitutions* 719 and 811)

The Prayer of the Lark

I am here! O my God.
I am here, I am here!
You draw me away from earth,
and I climb to You
in a passion of shrilling,
to the dot in heaven
where, for an instant, You crucify me.
When will you keep me forever?
Must You always let me fall
back to the furrow's dip,
a poor bird of clay?
Oh, at least
let my exultant nothingness
soar to the glory of Your mercy,
in the same hope,
until death.
Amen.

Carmen Bernos de Gasztold
translated by Rumer Godden

Week 22—The Spirit of Jesus

THEME: The Spirit is alive, working in the Church and in each of its members.

GRACE: I pray, joyfully and generously, for a deeper awareness of the presence and power of the Spirit of Jesus in all the events of my life.

PRAYER:
A. **John 16:5-15**
I recall the words of Jesus about the work of the Holy Spirit.

B. **Acts 2:1-21**
The promise of the Spirit's coming is fulfilled when the day of Pentecost arrived.

C. **Acts 10:44-48**
While Peter was speaking, the Holy Spirit came down upon all those who were listening. The work of evangelization had begun. I pray to embrace that work energetically.

D. **1 Corinthians 12:1-11**
Prayerfully I ask for a deepened faith in the gifts of the Holy Spirit.

E. **Repetition**

F. **Repetition**

G. **Application of the Senses**

Suggested Readings:

CONSTITUTIONS AND CONGREGATIONS: *The Account of Conscience*
General Examen 91-92, 93, 97
263, 424, 551
GC 31:271
GC 31:278-280
GC 32:116, 230-234
GC 32:249, 251
GC 32:256

[The Superior General] should know the consciences, as far as possible, of those whom he has in his charge. . . . Likewise, it should be strongly recommended to all that they should have and show great reverence, especially interior reverence, to their superiors, by considering and reverencing Jesus Christ in them; and from their hearts they should warmly love their superiors as fathers in Him. Thus in everything they should proceed in a spirit of charity, keeping nothing exterior or interior hidden from the superiors and desiring them to be informed about everything, in order that the superiors may be the better able to direct them in everything along the path of salvation and perfection. For that reason, once a year and as many times more as their superior thinks good, all the professed and formed coadjutors should be ready to manifest their consciences to him, in confession, or secret, or in another manner, for the sake of the great profit this practice contains.(*Constitutions* 764 and 551)

The dove descending breaks the air
With flame of incandescent terror
Of which the tongues declare
The one discharge from sin and error.
The only hope, or else despair
   Lies in the choice of pyre or pyre—
   To be redeemed from fire by fire.

Who then devised the torment? Love.
Love is the unfamiliar Name
Behind the hands that wove
The intolerable shirt of flame
Which human power cannot remove.
   We only live, only suspire
   Consumed by either fire or fire.

T. S. Eliot

Week 23—The Prodigal God

THEME: The Father, Son and Spirit are always at work sharing themselves with us. This sharing empowers us to become contemplatives-in-action, finding God in all things. "Each member of every Jesuit community is ever mindful of what Saint Ignatius says about love, that it consists in sharing what one has, what one is, and those one loves." (GC 32:28)

GRACE: I ask the Father to give me an intimate knowledge of the many gifts received, that filled with gratitude for all, I may in all things love and serve the Divine Majesty.

PRAYER: **A.** **Exercises 230-234.   Contemplatio Ad Amorem**
           The first point.

          B. **Exercises 230-233, 235.   Contemplatio Ad Amorem**
           The second point.

          C. **Exercises 230-233, 236.   Contemplatio Ad Amorem**
           The third point.

          D. **Exercises 230-233, 237.   Contemplatio Ad Amorem**
           The fourth point.

          E. **Repetition**

          F. **Repetition**

          G. **Application of the Senses**

Suggested Readings:

CONSTITUTIONS AND CONGREGATIONS: *The Union of Minds and Hearts*
GC 32, Decree 11

Whatever helps toward the union of the members of this Society among themselves and with their head will also help much toward preserving the well-being of the Society. This is especially the case with the bond of wills, which is the mutual charity and love they have for one another. (*Constitutions* 821)

Canticle of the Sun

Most high Lord,
Yours are the praises,
The glory and the honors,
And to you alone must be accorded
All graciousness; and no man there is
who is worthy to name you.
Be praised, O God, and be exalted
My Lord of all creatures,
And in especial of the most high Sun
Which is your creature, O Lord, that makes clear
The day and illumines it,
Whence by its fairness and its splendor
It is become thy face;
And of the white moon (be praised, O Lord)
And of the wandering stars,
Created by you in the heaven
So brilliant and so fair.
Praised be my Lord, by the flame
Whereby night groweth illumined
In the midst of its darkness,
For it is resplendent,
Is joyous, fair, eager; is mighty.
Praised be my Lord, of the air,
Of the winds, of the clear sky,
And of the cloudy, praised
Of all seasons whereby
Live all these creatures
Of lower order.
Praised be my Lord
By our sister the water,
Element meetest for man,
Humble and chaste in its clearness.

Praised be the Lord by our mother
The Earth that sustaineth,
That feeds, that produceth
Multitudinous grasses
And flowers and fruitage.
Praised be my Lord, by those
Who grant pardons through his love,
Enduring their travail in patience
And their infirmity with joy of the spirit.
Praised be my Lord by death corporal
Whence escapes no one living.
Woe to those that die in mutual transgression
And blessed are they who shall
Find in death's hour thy grace that comes
From obedience to thy holy will,
Wherethrough they shall never see
The pain of the death eternal.
Praise and give grace to my Lord
Be grateful and serve him
In humbleness e'en as ye are,
Praise him all creatures!

St. Francis of Assisi,
translated by Ezra Pound

Week 24—Totally in His Hands

THEME: At the close of his Exercises, Iñigo has successfully resolved the problem of his life. The service of God will be his ideal, Jesus Christ his model, the wide world his field of action. For from this moment he will no longer be the solitary pilgrim totally given to meditation and penance, but he will devote all his strength to "the help of souls," that is, to helping men to the fulfillment of their end. (Cándido de Dalmases, *St. Ignatius Loyola*, p. 69)

GRACE: I ask the Father for an intimate knowledge of the many gifts received, that filled with gratitude for all, I may in all things love and serve the Divine Majesty.

PRAYER: **A. Exercises 230-235. Contemplatio Ad Amorem**
I make these first two points by reviewing the graces and consolations of the First Week.

B. Exercises 230-235. Contemplatio Ad Amorem
I review the graces of the Second Week in the light of these points.

C. Exercises 230-233, 236-237. Contemplatio Ad Amorem
I make the third and fourth points by reviewing the graces and consolations of the Third Week.

D. Exercises 230-23, 236-237. Contemplatio Ad Amorem
I make the third and fourth points by reviewing the graces of the Fourth Week of the Exercises.

E. "Like St. Ignatius, I implore the Virgin Mary that we may all be placed with her Son; and that as Queen and Mother of the Society she be with us in all our labors." (Homily of Fr. Pedro Arrupe at La Storta, September 4, 1983)

We confidently call upon the intercession of the Queen and Mother of our Society for the complete fulfillment of (our) mission, imploring her with our Holy Father Saint Ignatius to intercede for us sinners with her Son and Lord and to obtain for us the grace so that, in conjunction with our own efforts, we may change from weak and sad individuals to strong and happy ones for the glory of God. (GC 33:55)

More than ever, I now find myself in the hands of God. This is what I have wanted all my life, from my youth. And this is still the one thing I want. But now there is a difference: the initiative is entirely with God. It is indeed a profound spiritual experience to know and feel myself so totally in his hands. (Message of Father Pedro Arrupe to the Society, September 3, 1983)

Take, Lord, and receive all my liberty,

my memory, my understanding, and my entire will,

all that I have and possess.

Thou hast given all to me.

To Thee, O Lord, I return it.

All is Thine, dispose of it wholly according to Thy will.

Give me Thy love and Thy grace,

for this is sufficient for me.